Fatal Sword

Tragic Clash of Two Friends
on Christmas Eve

David K. Dodd

BAY CREEK PUBLISHING

FATAL SWORD

August 2017

The events and descriptions in this book are true. For reasons of privacy, pseudonyms have been widely used. An asterisk (*) placed next to a name indicates a pseudonym and applies to that person throughout the book. Any resemblance of a pseudonym to the name of a real person, alive or dead, is purely coincidental.

Cover design by Patrick Fisher.

Library of Congress Control Number 2017951678

ISBN 978-0-9835670-4-2

Published by
Bay Creek Publishing
PO Box 221697
Saint Louis, MO 63122

Dedicated to the friends of
Tom* and Steve

Contents

Preface

After the terrorist attacks of September 11, 2001, all Americans were urged to perform their civic duty: BOLO—*be on the lookout*. Report any suspicious behavior to authorities. This official appeal seemed perplexing to residents of small towns like Sturgeon Bay, Wisconsin. *Terrorist attacks in our tiny town? We barely have a tower three stories high!* Sturgeon Bay had only six-thousand full-year residents, and the closest major city was 155 miles away. Still, the idea that terrorists could be lurking around any corner was unsettling.

Like most Americans, those in Sturgeon Bay undoubtedly had strong feelings about the terrorism of 9/11. Anger and disgust were voiced in conversations with neighbors and loved ones and in letters to local newspaper editors. But the reactions of two local residents in particular went far beyond typical or appropriate boundaries.

A few days after September 11, a resident called the Sturgeon Bay Police Department and spoke to Clerk Jenniece Hoiska. The caller was extremely upset: "Nobody goes and kills Americans and gets away with it." He then offered the police department his personal assistance, stating, "I should go get him myself," apparently referring to Osama bin Laden. The caller identified himself as Steve Owens.

Later that year, on December 17 or 18, a bar patron got into a heated confrontation with a fellow drinker at the Greystone Castle tavern in Sturgeon Bay, and the two nearly came to blows. Ten days later, when the patron heard about a murder investigation, he called police and described the bar room incident. "The guy's political views were very extreme, really different from most people's." The guy was Tom Azinger*.

Fatal Sword

Tom Azinger and Steve Owens had known each other casually for fifteen years and closely for seven years, drawn together by Greg Hoefman*, a best friend to each of them. Greg and Steve shared a modest apartment, and Tom lived with his mother, practically next door. When Tom appeared at the front door of the apartment on December 24, he looked forward to a relaxing evening with his friends. Instead, one of three died and, for the surviving two, life was irreparably changed. The families of the men would also be wounded forever.

The facts of this case are brutal, distressing, and heartbreaking. There is little controversy about *what* happened. The mystery is *why* it happened, and what the *intentions* of the friends were as they engaged in a fatal fight. A controversial trial did little to solve the puzzle and, in the eyes of some, provided scant justice.

I am aware that the events depicted in this book may renew painful memories for those closest to the tragedy. In an effort to guard their privacy, I have made liberal use of pseudonyms, denoted with an asterisk (*) upon their first occurrence. Specifically, pseudonyms are used for: Tom and his mother, former wives, and long-time girlfriend; Steve's mother and sister; Greg and his siblings and mother; and a few others who played principal roles in the story.

~ ~

When I first began writing this book, I set two goals: First, I wanted to humanize Tom Azinger and Steve Owens for readers. Second, I sought to tell their story as accurately and objectively as possible.

I asked a friendly acquaintance of mine, "If I say the name 'Tom Azinger,' do you know who that is?"

Though he had lived in the Sturgeon Bay area for many years, he looked at me blankly before responding, "No. Should I?"

Preface

"What about this? Do you remember someone being stabbed to death, about fifteen years ago?" I was determined to keep at it until he recalled something, *anything*.

"Oh, yeah. Some guy was at a drinking party and got killed with a samurai sword. I remember that!"

"Yes," I explained, "that guy was Tom Azinger, and the man who stabbed him was his friend, Steve Owens. Did you know either one of them?"

"No, but my family is distant relatives of the Azingers, I'm pretty sure."

Undoubtedly, my friend had read the same newspaper articles, fourteen years earlier, that I only recently discovered. He had forgotten almost everything about the case, just as I was beginning to study it. Many times I have re-read those articles—ten covering the trial alone, I found—and I realized why my friend had no memory of either Tom or Steve. The articles were good reports, perhaps, from the perspective of the reporters and their editors, who faced deadlines and word limits. But they seemed oversimplified and sensational, and frustrating in their sparsity of detail and analysis.

News about the trial focused primarily on the courtroom presentations of the attorneys and the most dramatic testimony of witnesses. At the forefront of the articles, and sometimes even in their headlines, was the vivid labeling of the fatal weapon as a "samurai sword." It is little wonder that casual followers of the trial remember the sword, but little if anything about Azinger and Owens.

Tom and Steve were friends. They shared experiences together and had mutual friends. Each struggled during their adults lives. Aware of the other's faults, they generally accepted each other, for the sake of friendship. Their tragic ending deserves a far better telling than what was presented in short news stories. To grasp fully what happened on that fateful Christmas Eve in 2001 requires understanding the personal complexities of Tom and Steve.

Fatal Sword

I introduce the trial of Steve Owens early in the book, so readers can begin to experience the case in roughly the same way jurors did. Then I intersperse chapters detailing the lives of Tom and Steve with the remainder of the trial. These chapters provide important information unavailable to the jury, especially critical events leading up to the disastrous evening. In the end, readers themselves will have the opportunity to judge what happened, and whether justice was served.

1

Eve

In late afternoon, three friends came together at the apartment shared by two of them. Tom politely knocked at the front door, though his friends would never have objected if he walked in on his own. Tom hoped to spend Christmas Eve with Greg, and probably Steve would be there as well. Tom and Greg had been best friends since high school, while Tom and Steve had known each other for fifteen years, due to their mutual friendship with Greg.

Steve was forty, the other two about three years younger. They shared a passion for guitars, and for drinking. All three were known to abuse alcohol, Tom and Greg habitually and Steve occasionally. Tom arrived at the apartment with his guitar and two-thirds of a large bottle of brandy. If there were not enough drink to get them through the evening, he'd worry about it later.

All three men were close to their families, all nearby. Steve planned to spend the following day—Christmas—with his mother, sister, and nephews. Tom turned down an invitation to join his family's large, Christmas Eve celebration, which would include his mother, three adult siblings, and nieces and nephews.

Greg, on the other hand, was planning to spend the early evening with his own family. In fact, he was practically walking out the front door as Tom arrived. He looked forward to seeing his family—his brother, sister, and parents—but now that Tom had arrived, Greg also wanted to spend time with his best buddies. He told Tom and Steve he would be back in a couple of hours. It was a promise he didn't keep.

Fatal Sword

During the next five hours, Tom and Steve passed the time by playing videogames, eating snacks, smoking marijuana, and drinking. For most of the evening, the television was on with the volume muted, a visual distraction rather than a source of entertainment. And then the guitars came out.

Steve was a fantastic player, but Tom was just learning. Tom's guitar needed new strings and a repair, and Steve readily offered his expertise. Unfortunately, things took a wrong turn—a rusty screw refused to loosen, leaving the guitar's bridge unfixable and both men feeling defeated. Frustration spilled over into a silly dispute about 9/11, which quickly led to a brawl, a fatal blow, and a desperate call to 9-1-1. One friend died, another was charged with intentional homicide, and the third was caught in the middle, stupefied by it all.

2

Judges

The trial of Steve D. Owens began on Monday, July 23, 2002, in the Door County courtroom of Judge Peter C. Diltz. Owens was charged with first-degree intentional homicide for the death of Tom Azinger seven months earlier, on Christmas Eve 2001. Representing the state of Wisconsin was District Attorney Tim W. Funnell. Sitting "second chair" for the prosecution was Lt. Thomas Baudhuin, a long-time officer and investigator for the Sturgeon Bay Police Department. Baudhuin had responded immediately to the 911 call following Azinger's stabbing, and he was closely involved in all aspects of the case, including the crime scene and the suspect's arrest and interrogation. He was also in charge of maintaining the security of key evidence, most notably the sword used in the fatal event.

At the defense table was Nila J. Robinson, along with her longtime assistant, private investigator Gary Smith. Rounding out the ensemble were Judge Diltz and Owens, the defendant. The stage was set, except for the empty jury box.

Seventy-five Door County residents responded to the call for jury duty, with Judge Diltz noting his displeasure at five who failed to show up. The key objective of Day 1 of the trial was finding twelve jurors, plus two alternates, who could be absolutely "fair and impartial." With all potential jurors seated in the courtroom, twenty-eight were randomly selected to take positions at the front. The judge began by delivering the perjury admonishment: "Do each of you understand and agree to answer all questions accurately and truthfully, under penalty of perjury and being subject to criminal prosecution?" Whether out of civic duty, following the pack, or pure fear, all seventy-five readily agreed.

"Does anyone know defense attorney Nila Robinson? Raise your hands." No one did. "What about her assistant, Gary Smith?" Again, there was no response.

"How about prosecutor Tim Funnell? Does anyone know him?" Almost every hand shot up. Taken aback, Diltz re-phrased: "Well, since he *is* an elected official, most people will know him, so it makes sense. The question is: Can you be fair and impartial?" The potential jurors were happy to explain—perhaps even boast a little—about how they knew Funnell. "I'm in Optimist's Club with Mr. Funnell." "My husband works with Mr. Funnell in Challenge Program [an alternative program for at-risk students]." "Tim shoots on our company team." "I know his wife." "I played baseball against Tim Funnell." "My parents know his parents, but it's no big deal."

This "no big deal" comment was what Diltz seemed to pick up on. "Yes, it is a small community, so naturally 'everybody knows everybody.' But the issue is whether knowing Mr. Funnell prevents anyone from being fair and impartial. Is there anyone who cannot be fair and impartial?" He paused for hands to rise. Seeing none, he moved on.

Diltz then listed the names of five persons likely to be witnesses for the prosecution. Among them were Lorine Azinger* and several police officers. "Who might know any of these witnesses?" the judge inquired.

"I used to work with Lorine, but that's been over fifteen years ago." "My mom was friends with Lorine Azinger and they played cards together, but that was years ago." "My dad owns property next to hers, and my aunt is Lorine's niece."

One man noted that he "graduated high school in 1998" with Officer [Carl] Waterstreet. Then several piped in that they too knew Waterstreet, as well as Officer Wendy Allen. Another reported, "I work hand-in-hand with the fire and police, so I know about every officer." Judge Diltz was beginning to feel like voir dire was turning into a bragging contest. He was eager to keep things moving but was obliged to list another five prosecution witnesses. Predictably, they were also well-known around town.

Particularly prominent was potential witness Tom Austad, an emergency medical technician who would later testify about being on the scene on December 24. Austad was a well-liked local resident who, with his brother, owned and ran a hardware store in the middle of town. Virtually anyone who had ever purchased hardware knew Tom. The potential jurors didn't hold back, including one who admitted she had dated Tom's nephew. Rivaling Austad's popularity was Officer Tim Fuerst. "He was my baseball coach!" "My daughter used to date him, years ago." On and on it went.

Finally, the judge read the last eight names of witnesses for the prosecution. Knowing that one of them, Gary Rabach, was a long-time police officer and a football coach at the high school, Diltz seemed to cringe in anticipation of all the connections that would be forthcoming. Other significant names that brought instant recognition were police officers Arleigh Porter, Thomas Baudhuin, and Terry Vogel.

Judge Diltz tried his best to maintain order and keep things progressing, without stifling those who wanted to express their connections to witnesses. His common refrain was, "But you can set that aside and still be fair and impartial, can't you?" A few persisted, stating in effect, "I cannot be impartial." By mid-morning, seven of them had been excused by the judge and their seats filled by other potential jurors from the back of the room.

Next it was time to get to the probable witnesses for the defense. Public defender Robinson was prepared to call at least ten witnesses, and their names were read. Some worked for the police department, and again, many potential jurors had connections with them. One key witness for the defense, who also happened to be a witness for the prosecution, was Greg Hoefman, best friend to both the victim and the defendant. Greg was well-known around Sturgeon Bay, partly because of his winning personality but also as a talented guitarist who played at various local venues. The connections followed: "Greg is my dad's first cousin." "I used to work with Greg." "I know Greg, as well as his sister and cousin" (who were also potential witnesses).

Finally it was time to examine any connections to the victim and defendant. Does anyone know Tom Azinger or Steve Owens? Only a few did. "I'm associated with both of them, because my husband knew them in high school." More meaningfully, another admitted, "I'm friends with Steve's nephew and we've discussed this case." That was enough for Judge Diltz, who excused her.

Diltz continued. "Has anybody heard about or discussed this case? Probably most of you have, since it's been in the papers." He was right—practically everyone knew about the stabbing death, and many admitted discussing the details "over coffee." But no one admitted to having already formed an opinion that would prevent the rendering of a fair and impartial verdict.

The next queries were about illnesses requiring forthcoming treatment and about major personal commitments, such as planned vacations. When a few hands went up, Judge Diltz wanted to know details. Then he tried his best to eliminate conflicts, even offering to call to a physician's office to help change the date of a standing appointment.

Finally it was time to shift from group voir dire in the courtroom to individual voir dire in the judge's chamber. Instead of directing questions to the whole group and relying on each potential juror to volunteer information, the individual questioning was more focused and required a specific response. Always the focus was on the person's background, knowledge of the defendant and witnesses, and exposure to prior information about the case. A few participants insisted they could not be impartial, and they were released from duty.

Judges

At some point during the individual voir dire, public defender Nila Robinson complained: "Judge, you're asking the jurors a lot of leading questions. For example, asking 'But you can still be fair and impartial, can't you?' makes it easy for them to give the answer you are hoping for." The judge was open to the criticism, responding, "That is not my intention. If I do it again, let me know."

Individual voir dire continued for hours until the questioning of the last person was completed—finally! Prosecutor Tim Funnell himself seemed to be running out of gas, as he reminded the judge, "It's 5:30 right now." Nila Robinson had her own opinion: "Let's just go ahead and finish up." The lawyers, judge, and defendant returned to the courtroom, where the potential jurors were waiting.

"Has anybody ever been on a jury before?" Funnell asked. It was a question essential to determining whether prior experience might affect one's ability to be fair. Clearly the audience was growing weary, as responses were brief and agreeable. Next, Robinson reminded everyone that the burden of proof was on the *state,* not the defense, and that the criterion was proof beyond a reasonable doubt. Everyone seemed to understand and agree.

At 6:00 p.m. the judge, lawyers, and defendant returned to the judge's chamber. Each side was allowed four preemptive strikes and the judge had a few of his own. Twenty minutes later they returned to the courtroom, and their final selections were announced. Those not chosen were roundly thanked by the judge and excused from further duty, leaving fourteen to be sworn in as jurors. Judge Diltz gave a detailed admonition about what the jurors could and could not do on their own time. Then he dismissed them, with the instruction: "We will start tomorrow at 8:30 a.m. Don't be late." The clock read 6:40 p.m. Day 1 had been long and exhausting.

3
Benchmarks

Most of the jurors grew up in or around Door County. Like almost every other denizen of "The Door," they loved the beauty of the wide-open waters and arborous state parks. They were proud that so many tourists appreciated their area, though they often felt annoyed by inconveniences imposed by the seasonal influx.

Residents boast of their peaceful small towns and the area's low crime rate, characteristics that help draw tourists by the thousands from Chicago, Milwaukee, Madison and, just an hour away, Green Bay. Ask locals about serious crime and you might get the response, "We don't have many murders in Door County, but when we do, they're *doozies!*"

In fact, sensational homicides are a big part of the local history. Jurors in the Steve Owens case were surely aware of such cases, either directly or from stories handed down by parents and grandparents. Storytellers often use hyperbole to spice things up, but the dramatic murders from Door County's past need no enhancement.

When the jurors received their report notices in the spring of 2002, they might have guessed the trial of Steve Owens was on the horizon, and their speculations were quickly confirmed during jury selection. Were they about to become a part of yet another sensational local case? Would they someday tell their children and grandchildren stories about their role as jurors in the case of the fatal "Samurai sword"?

~ ~

Benchmarks

In 1948, Mrs. Sadie Cody was killed just inside the front door of her mansion near downtown Sturgeon Bay, Wisconsin. She was one of the town's wealthiest and best-known residents and, at age eighty-five, one of the oldest. She died as a consequence of a punch to the face by her fifty-year-old tenant, Bill Drews. There was also a fiery furnace involved, which helped explain the nation-wide attention drawn to the case. A seven-day manhunt produced near hysteria in the small community but ended in the arrest of Drews.

After a vigorous, eight-hour interrogation, Drews confessed. He later recanted, though it made little difference. The trial lasted just two days, with Drews's public defender putting up practically no defense. The jury took only sixty-eight minutes to return with its verdict—*guilty of murder in the first degree.* The next day Bill Drews was transported to the state penitentiary to begin serving his life sentence.

Harvey Rowe, as the fourteen-year-old son of the local sheriff, witnessed practically everything and, as an adult, wrote a lengthy manuscript about the intriguing case. Years after Harvey's death in 2003, I adapted his manuscript into *Furnace Murder,* published in 2014. The case still evokes fascination among local residents, and the mansion is a stop on a popular "Ghost Tour" of the town. Many who were children and teenagers in the 1950s and 1960s attended parties or dances at "Mrs. Cody's," which had been bequeathed to a fraternal organization.

~ ~

In 1953, Sumner and Grace Harris were killed inexplicably by the boy next door. The Harrises were prominent and popular citizens of Sturgeon Bay, true civic leaders, and the entire community mourned their deaths. Adding to the intrigue was that the fourteen-year-old was home on summer vacation from St. Joseph's Seminary in Milwaukee, Wisconsin, where he was studying for the priesthood. He was struggling academically, however, and was ineligible to return in the fall.

By all accounts, the boy was fond of the Harrises, and vice versa. They had employed him to mow their lawn and do odd jobs. When he went to the Harrises' back door at 7:30 p.m. and knocked, Grace naturally let him in. He killed her and waited two hours for her husband to arrive home from his work as publisher of the county newspaper. When Sumner appeared, the boy immediately stabbed him to death. He returned home and left a brief confession note to his mother, saying "I killed Mr. and Mrs. H. Call the police and tell them I'm heading to Michigan." His younger sister heard him leave the home and start what she thought was the family car. In fact, he stole the Harrises' car and fled toward Illinois.

The bodies of Sumner and Grace Harris lay in their living room for twelve hours before being found the following morning. The discovery quickly became a community event, with people walking all over the crime scene. "People" included local citizens, reporters, and of course the local police. A photographer finally suggested that the police seal off the crime seen, which they did, but not before the murder weapon—a bloody hunting knife—was handled by numerous onlookers.

Less than twenty-four hours after committing the double murder, the youngster was captured in Indiana. Although lacking a driver's license, he had managed to drive the getaway car hundreds of miles before eventually losing control and running it into a ditch. He began walking and ended up sleeping on the dirt floor of a public restroom at the county courthouse. The next morning he was discovered and arrested for vagrancy, with only a dollar in his pocket. Local authorities found the disabled Harris car and, having heard of the nationwide manhunt, put two and two together and contacted Wisconsin officials. Door County Sheriff Hallie Rowe, along with his son Harvey, traveled to Indiana and returned the boy to his hometown.

Benchmarks

Almost immediately the boy confessed to killing the Harrises. He claimed to have gagged and tied up Grace before she escaped in about twenty minutes and attempted to call the police. That's when he said he stabbed her to death. Curiously, the autopsy revealed that Grace died of strangulation, with the knife wounds coming later. There was, however, no doubt about *Sumner's* death—it was a brutal stabbing. What drove the boy to kill? Everyone was dying for an answer, but even the boy could not explain it: "I don't know why I did it . . . something upstairs told me to do it."

The boy was two months short of his fifteenth birthday, and his case was handled within the "secret and protective confines of the juvenile court." In other words, there was no public record of what happened to the youth. Newspapers reported he was transferred to the "state boys home," to be held until he turned twenty-one, when he would be released and his youth record expunged. There was public outrage at the leniency, especially when it became known that the facility had no walls to prevent the wards from just walking away and again terrorizing their local towns.

The boy did, in fact, just walk away, but not until he turned twenty-one and was officially released. His future? He became a law-abiding citizen—a father and grandfather—albeit hundreds of miles from Sturgeon Bay. Understandably he sought anonymity. According to one local citizen, even the man's wife did not learn of her husband's grisly past until she had been married to him for decades.

~ ~

In 1996, David Dellis choked a friend to death during an argument. Dellis thought Mike had just passed out, but when he never came to, Dellis transported the body from Brown County, Wisconsin, to Carl Whitford's farm in southern Door County. Dellis's macabre plan was to hide the evidence by sawing Mike up into thirty-two parts and burning him in a trash barrel. He accomplished the first part and was cleaning up his saw when three people came upon the scene. Dellis fled, leaving the passersby to discover Mike's parts in the barrel.

Dellis headed north twenty miles to a rural area near Baileys Harbor. There he lay low for several days in an unoccupied farmhouse. When the owners—an elderly couple—returned home, he tied them up, stole their money, and took off in their truck. Thirsty, he stopped at a popular watering hole—the Coyote Roadhouse—where he blundered decisively. Asked for identification before he could be served, Dellis produced a *library card,* with his own name on it! While the bartender was sorting things out, Dellis fled in the truck. The bartender immediately alerted authorities.

Within an hour Dellis was apprehended by Terry Vogel, the same officer who interrogated Steve Owens five years later. Dellis was read his Miranda rights, then confessed. Authorities in Brown County, where the strangulation occurred, gladly transferred the gory case to Door County, and it landed in the court of Judge Peter Diltz. District Attorney Greg J. Schuster, the predecessor to Tim Funnell, threw a slew of felony charges at Dellis, nine in all (eventually whittled down to six).

To rule out insanity Dellis was examined and found competent to stand trial, though psychological disturbances were noted. With an insanity plea no longer viable, it was time for plea-bargaining. Negotiations were so complex that two separate hearings were required. Most notably, the original charge of second-degree reckless homicide, for choking Mike, was reduced to negligent homicide *by use of a dangerous weapon.* It was the best that Dellis's attorney could do. Both sides stipulated that no "dangerous weapon" was ever involved—David's hands didn't count. The State gained from the deal because it would have had difficulty proving the original charge of second-degree reckless homicide. The defense gained by a reduction of the felony from Class C to Class D.

After the plea bargaining was finally over, David Dellis was sentenced to thirty-two years of imprisonment for his crimes in 1996. He is eligible for parole in 2017 and his mandatory release date (for extended, community supervision) is 2018. He will be "free and clear" of all supervision in 2028.

~ ~

Over the years there have been other homicides in Door County, but none is so burned into the collective memory of residents as are the Cody, Harris, and Dellis cases. Steven Owens, naturally, knew of the area's history of crime. In fact, he himself had even lived on the Whitford farm, about two years before David Dellis made it famous. As he came to trial, he might have sensed that his name might unfortunately be the next to become part of local legend.

4

Youths

Steve Owens was born in Milwaukee, Wisconsin, in 1961. His family lived in a modest house in a working class neighborhood on the city's northwest side. Parents Bill and Iona* were born in the years shortly before World War II, married in the late 1950s, and started their family shortly thereafter.

Bill had pursued a career as a mechanic in the air force, before retiring and entering the civilian work force. Soon after, he met Iona and their dreams turned toward marriage and children. Bill worked hard as a mechanic, determined to provide the material necessities his young family needed. Iona had held clerical positions but was more than content to become a full-time mother and homemaker. The couple was ready to expand, and so they did. First came Dawn*, then fourteen months later, Steve.

Steve's early years in Milwaukee were mostly uneventful. He had few friends but was not necessarily lonely. His interests gravitated to science and nature. One might assume that "nature" was hard to find in a large city like Milwaukee, but Steve had no difficulty finding beauty and solitude—his favorite refuge was a mere few blocks from his house. Alongside railroad tracks was a preserve, of sorts, land owned by the railroad but available for all, including eleven-year-old explorers.

Steve's best memories of Milwaukee were the hours and hours he spent at the preserve, walking about, investigating a small stream, bird-watching with binoculars, and enjoying the beautiful, endless sky. Spotting a mammal of any kind thrilled him. Nature was the draw, but something else was pushing him. Steve felt cramped in his small home, in his crowded neighborhood, and in school, where his classmates seemed indifferent toward him, if not unkind. At the preserve Steve could breathe deeply and feel alive.

Bill, on the other hand, became increasingly concerned that a big city was not the best place to raise kids. Was it the worsening of nearby crime, or his growing unrest? Either way, he heard a voice telling him, *Move on!*

As head of the household, Bill made the decision to relocate his family to a safer, more wholesome area. He found a well-paying job in the shipbuilding industry in Sturgeon Bay, Wisconsin, and in 1973 moved his family to a rural home near Brussels, about ten miles from Sturgeon Bay. Steve was twelve, in the middle of his sixth-grade year.

Presumably, Iona, Dawn, and Steve were in agreement with Bill's decision, or at least could appreciate his reasoning. Steve hated to leave behind the railroad preserve that was his "center" as he entered adolescence. Yet moving to Brussels offered a new start. A new school meant making friends and gaining acceptance, hopefully.

Steve quickly became friends with Patrick Jeanquart, a farm boy who was liked but not really popular. Patrick was as straight as a rail on a new fence. His teachers, much more than his classmates, appreciated his calm, obedient nature.

Patrick recalls one of his first memories of Steve. It was in sixth-grade homeroom, possibly Steve's first day in school. The teacher dutifully introduced Steve to the class and asked him the easiest question she could think of. "Tell us, what were some things your family did while you lived in Milwaukee?" Steve didn't hesitate. "One day we went to the zoo and some hoodlums took bricks from the sidewalk and threw them at the hippos!" The teacher was aghast, but the story thrilled Steve's new classmates. The eyes of the girls widened, while the boys hooted—some even applauded. Clearly Steve had picked the right story to impress his peers.

Fatal Sword

Patrick remembers another story. At recess a group of boys asked Steve more about his life in Milwaukee, and someone asked, "What did your dad do there?" Steve pictured his dad trudging off every morning to his job as a commercial mechanic, a job that would hardly dazzle his audience. So he answered, "My dad was a *street fighter!*" Needless to say, the boys were wildly fascinated, though they may have had little idea what a "street fighter" really was.

Steve made some friends and some enemies. The "new kid from Milwaukee" was viewed as exotic, not just because of the stories he told but because he seemed eccentric. What fascinated some seemed to irk others, who viewed Steve as a braggart and an outsider. Plus, he was the smallest boy in sixth-grade, not an enviable distinction. Predictably he got into arguments and occasional fights.

Steve liked getting noticed by teachers, that is, the ones that gave him positive attention. Other teachers, though, seemed to have it in for Steve. He was constantly doing artwork instead of homework, annoying his teachers who tried to keep him on task. His first drawings were clumsy and drew the ridicule of his classmates. But Steve kept at it and, with practice and occasional help from a peer, his art improved rapidly.

Steve had one skill that was greatly admired by all his schoolmates, particularly the boys. His dad had taught him to whistle loudly and shrilly, by putting two fingers in his mouth, just right. Though many asked him to teach them the technique, none could master it like Steve. On one memorable occasion, Steve exhibited his talent, uninvited, at a school concert. His friends went wild, but a nearby teacher escorted Steve out by the nape of his neck.

Steve was getting acclimated to his new school, but what he enjoyed most about his new life was the wide-open spaces surrounding his country home. Instead of a narrow strip of railroad preserve like the one in Milwaukee, he now had access to wide-open fields, woods, and creeks of all sizes.

Youths

The evening sky was something he had never experienced. Of course, Milwaukee had a sky but it was muted by constant, all-night city lights. In Brussels Steve found, for the first time, a fascinating sky with bountiful stars and wondrous constellations. He was closer to the heavens than he had ever been.

Steve's family lived in a rented farmhouse a few miles north of Brussels, and Patrick remembers visiting regularly. The Owens parents genuinely seemed to enjoy Steve's friends and Patrick made himself at home, though the dynamics of the Owens family seemed different from his own. Steve's father could be somewhat bombastic, while his mother was cautious and deathly afraid of spiders. Removing all insects and webs from the living quarters was Steve's daily chore. On laundry day he descended into the basement with a vacuum to clear out any conceivable presence of spiders, eventually calling out, "No cobwebs in the basement!" Only then would his mother head down to do the laundry.

According to Patrick, Steve was allowed to argue with his parents. Sometimes Steve chose drawing over completing his chores, and this could cause arguments. The father would occasionally throw Steve's artwork across the room, but there was never anything more physical than that. Once when Steve was arguing with his mother, things came to a head. He walked over to a closet and challenged his mother, "There's a rifle in there, why don't you get it and just shoot me!" That was enough to rattle the mother and bring the conflict to a close.

In the fall of 1976, Steve entered Southern Door High School as a freshman. He and Patrick tried out for the football team. Steve hated sports, but in an effort to gain acceptance, he tried out anyway and made the freshman squad. He and Patrick were now teammates! A big farm boy, Patrick found some playing time as a lineman, but Steve rarely played. "I was too small! They never gave me a chance." So much for his goal of social acceptance.

Fatal Sword

By the end of November, Steve's football career was over before it had hardly begun. His dad told the family they would soon be moving closer to Sturgeon Bay, and Steve and Dawn would be transferring high schools. Feeling like he never really fit in at Southern Door, Steve didn't care, though he hated leaving his friend Patrick. He told his pal about the move but asked him to keep it a secret. Being bullied was an ongoing issue for Steve, and he didn't want to give his nemeses one final crack at him.

At his new high school Steve hoped not for acceptance but mere anonymity. The more he sought invisibility, the more others noticed. He was "the kid from Milwaukee," a foreigner, of sorts. In addition, he was transferring in from Southern Door, the rival school mocked as "Cow Pie High." Besides being an outsider, Steve came across as being very different. He was small, wore unstylish clothes, and when he chose to speak up, expressed some pretty odd ideas. The bullying in his new school was even worse.

Steve remembers an incident that occurred within a week or two of his arrival at Sturgeon Bay. "This kid Dave—a freshman—slammed me against a panel of lockers. I was tired of being hassled, so I challenged him in P.E. I begged the coach, 'Give me and Dave ten minutes on the mat, just ten minutes!'" The coach turned his back, implicitly granting the boys' wish. Within a minute and a half, both boys had damaged noses and busted lips, and Dave was bleeding from the forehead. They decided to call it a draw, though both won each other's respect. "We became friends! For a while, at least, then we weren't."

It didn't help that Steve's main interests were art and science, rather than sports. In art class, his budding talent attracted the attention of his teacher, Mr. Roberts, who provided the extra instruction and praise Steve seemed to crave. Steve also loved his freshman science class and thrived under his watchful teacher, Mr. Hauser. When it came to extracurricular activities, Steve was disappointed

Youths

the school had no art club, but he readily joined the camera club, sponsored by Mr. Roberts, and also the science club.

These two clubs and classes were true havens for Steve, where he felt proficient and appreciated, where he could relax and be himself. The problem for Steve, though, was the time between classes and before and after school. He felt perpetually bullied by larger classmates and upperclassmen. Being taunted was part of his everyday experience and, if he dared to strike back in anyway, things could get physical, as it had in PE class.

One particular nemesis was nicknamed Banjo*, an accomplished athlete who wasn't content to rest on his laurels in sports. He enjoyed putting down smaller kids—weaklings, in his eyes—particularly Steve Owens. In art class Steve had drawn a large picture of Cheryl Tiegs, America's first supermodel. Along with the art of other students, Steve's drawing was prominently displayed in a school hallway. To his great dismay Steve learned his drawing had been almost immediately defaced with a thick, black marker. Finding the culprit was no problem—Banjo was bragging about it all over school.

Weeks later Steve was in study hall, putting final touches on an ethereal drawing of outer space. He felt it was his finest drawing, with rich coloring and imaginative constellations, but to Banjo it was nothing but an invitation. Walking up to Steve's table, the bully loaded and spat right on the artwork. Steve reacted by leaping to his feet and punching him in the nose. Banjo got a trip to the hospital, and Steve got a three-day school suspension.

Steve continued to be the brunt of bullying, even as he approached his senior year. The classroom was bad enough, but the hallways and locker room were brutal. Sometimes teachers tried to squelch the bullying but often they did not, even seeming to offer tacit approval. Finally, Steve had had enough and he armed himself with a baseball bat. It is not clear if he merely brandished the bat or actually connected with his targets. Either way, he received another three-day suspension.

Besides science and art, Steve enjoyed his computer science class at school. It takes some imagination, perhaps, to picture a computer class in the late-1970s. The "mouse," a novel device at the time, was called an "x,y position indicator," or a "track ball mouse."

Instead of browsing the internet or sending emails, computer students communicated with the mainframe computer via punch cards and "code," while continuing to communicate with classmates in the usual way—verbally. But Steve not only mastered code, he cracked into the school administration's passwords. From there, he discovered a way to communicate with the computer at Southern Door High, miles away, where his friend Patrick was also enrolled in computer class.

"I began receiving cryptic computer messages from Steve," Patrick recalls. "Run program, print, kill program, push return." Some messages were humorous and referred to Monty Python, a television show the boys watched religiously. "RUN ALPHA ORION – It's a communist takeover. PLEASE DESTROY!"

Patrick found it all to be amazing and amusing. "Those might have been the first emails ever sent in Door County!" Steve was clearly breaching school information that was "classified," though harmless—class rosters, mostly. Nevertheless, Steve's antics earned him Patrick's considerable admiration. And a permanent suspension from computer lab.

~ ~

The summer after freshman year, Steve and Patrick decided to get jobs together at the local cherry processing plant in Sturgeon Bay. It was a marvelous opportunity for fifteen-year-olds—the pay was great and they worked alongside other teens, even classmates. It was lucrative if tedious work, but luckily they arranged to work the same shift.

The job came with drawbacks, however. First, Patrick lived in rural Brussels, more than fifteen miles away. Neither Steve nor Patrick had a driver's license, so they rode their bikes to work. Second, their shift lasted until about 2 a.m. Patrick could hardly be expected to bike all the way to Brussels in the middle of the night, so his family worked out an arrangement with the Owens family. Patrick spent three weeks staying with Steve, returning home only on days off. Dutifully, Patrick paid a small amount from his paycheck—room and board.

Patrick felt entirely welcome at the Owens home, though there were occasional rough spots. On the first night of the arrangement, the boys arrived home at about 3 a.m. and were greeted not by Steve's parents, but by the family dogs. The loud barking woke the parents, and the father, in particular, was highly displeased. The next night the boys avoided the dogs by sleeping in the Owens family car. This time it was Steve's mother who complained: "Wake up! I've got to go to work! And what are you doing in my car?"

The boys didn't mind the five-mile, late-night commute from the factory to Steve's house. The freedom of riding their bikes full-speed through town and into the country—it could be exhilarating! And occasionally dangerous.

One memorable night their ride home took an unexpected turn. The boys had just been paid, and with checks in their pockets, they headed home, hungry and eager to raid the refrigerator. But a drizzle became a downpour by the time the boys hit the Michigan St. Bridge—known historically as the Steel Bridge. Connecting Sturgeon Bay's east and west sides, the two-lane bridge is narrow, and bikers share an elevated sidewalk with pedestrians, not that there were any walkers in the middle of that rainy night.

Of the two boys, Patrick was cautious, Steve downright daring. The conditions were slick, so Patrick held back, but

Steve, showing off a little, sped ahead and reached the Steel Bridge well ahead of Patrick. Across the bridge he flew until he reached the west side, where he leaned into the sharp curve in the sidewalk. By the time Patrick reached the west end of the bridge, he was shocked to see his friend sitting in the backseat of a police cruiser, as an officer was putting Steve's bike into the trunk. It took a while for Patrick to grasp the harrowing story Steve told him.

As Steve took the curve at full speed, out of nowhere a police cruiser appeared, completely blocking the slick sidewalk. No doubt the officer was on the lookout for speeding *autos,* not bicycles. Steve tried to stop, though he knew wet brakes would be useless. He slammed into the rear quarter panel of the squad car. The bike crumpled, while the biker went flying over the car's trunk, like a gymnast performing an aerial flip. The officer got out of his squad car and came to the rescue. Scrappy Steve, lifting himself off the ground, shrugged off his scrapes and developing bruises and focused instead on his damaged bike—it was destroyed.

From this point, two very different versions of the story emerge. Patrick, a "gentle giant" then and now, is polite, respectful to authority, and mild-mannered, like an Eagle Scout. Here is his version: The officer was extremely attentive to Steve and concerned about his injuries. He offered to drive Steve home and did so—Steve in the back of the cruiser, the bike in the slightly damaged trunk. There was no room for both Patrick and his bike, so Patrick agreeably rode his bike on to Steve's house, arriving some time after Steve had been delivered by the helpful cop.

The next morning Bill Owens was already up when the boys crawled out of bed. "What happened to your bike, son?" Steve gave the basics of the accident while Patrick filled in the gaps. "The officer couldn't have been nicer, Mr. Owens. He checked Steve out, asked if he was okay, and even offered to take him to the hospital. Then he drove Steve home. By the time I got to your house, the officer was gone." Mr.

Youths

Owens's response was, "Oh, I *bet* he was friendly, he's hoping we don't sue him."

Steve's version of the incident: Immediately after the collision, the officer got out of his cruiser and carefully inspected its rear end, assessing the damage. He asked if Steve was all right, then he left. Steve had to walked home, carrying his demolished bike, while Patrick rode slowly alongside. The next day they discussed the incident with Steve's dad. His dad was worried the police department would try to sue for damages to the squad car, and a bill actually *was* sent to the Owenses, who ignored it.

~ ~

During the next school year Steve and Patrick remained friends from different schools, and they graduated from being cherry workers to young aviators. Patrick had saved enough from his summer earnings to buy a glider for $400. Steve could contribute nothing to the purchase but volunteered for the role of "chief mechanic."

The boys had great times trying to fly the glider, the emphasis on *trying*. First, they attempted to get the glider airborne by roping it to a tractor—Patrick drove while Steve piloted—but they could barely get any lift at all. Next, they hauled the glider up a steep hill and tried a running takeoff, again with disappointing results. A few weeks later Patrick turned sixteen and got his driver's license, so the boys tried pulling the glider behind a truck. "Steve was occasionally able to get the glider into the air, maybe six or eight feet, but I never could. Of course, I outweighed him by sixty pounds."

The boys uproariously celebrated their modest successes, which were far outnumbered by failures. "Thank goodness Steve knew how to make repairs," Patrick explained, "because I was worthless as his assistant. He'd use scrap metal, aluminum conduit, *anything* to get our glider back in service." Years later the glider was history—chopped up and discarded—but both boys were left with fond memories. And

Steve still has chronic neck pain to remind him of those youthful escapades.

~ ~

While Steve was suffering through his senior year at Sturgeon Bay, three other boys—all of whom would become important to Steve in adulthood—were beginning high school at a rival high school, six miles to the north. Sevastopol school district combines all of its twelve grades in a single building in the tiny town of Institute. At the time, a nearby parochial school annually graduated 10–12 eighth-grade students, most of whom transferred into Sevastopol High. In the fall of 1979, one of those students who "came over" was Tom Azinger.

The youngest of four siblings, Tom was raised on a farm a couple of miles from Institute. Like most "farm kids" he grew up enjoying a lot of freedom and fresh air, along with the drudgery of daily chores.

Greg Hoefman also grew up on a farm, a few miles north of the Azinger home. Brother Ricky*, one year younger, was exactly Tom Azinger's age, while sister Becki* was two years behind them. Their father was a dairy farmer when the children were small, and Ricky recalls how hard the kids worked. "As early as I can remember, I was lifting hay bales that weighed more than me!"

A few years later Mr. Hoefman decided to change occupations. If there's a job harder than dairy farming, it's commercial fishing, and that's what the dad chose. So Greg, Ricky, and Becki all learned fishing at a young age, and the boys spent much of their youth on the family's fishing vessel. It was taxing and often dangerous work, but Ricky caught the habit and, after his father retired, took over the business. Besides fishing, he got ensnared in another, lifelong habit. "When I was only eight, a crew member got me hooked—on cigarettes!"

Youths

The Azinger and Hoefman children all rode the same school bus, even in grade school, so they were well acquainted even before high school. By their high school years, there might have been as many as six children from the two families in different grades in the large, brick school building. Veteran teachers came to expect having an Azinger or Hoefman in their classes every year.

Tom loved most sports, especially football, which rewarded his "rough and tumble" nature. During freshman year he played football, baseball, and basketball. Conversely, the Hoefman boys did not find sports appealing. They worked hard for their dad and had no time for after-school practices or weekend games. But Tom and the Hoefman boys found other common interests.

Sevastopol's Conservation Club was founded and sponsored by the school superintendent, and it was a vibrant and popular club. Started in the early 1970s, spawned perhaps by Earth Day and the nascent environmental movement, Conservation Club attracted a wide variety of students and quickly grew into one of the school's most popular organizations. On field trips a full-sized bus was routinely filled to capacity by students eager for learning, fun, or just a day away from school. It was widely known some students—the partiers—lay claim to the back of the bus. There they could get away with smoking, if they were discreet about it, and even sip booze or take quick puffs of marijuana. Greg, Tom, and Ricky routinely gravitated to the back of the bus.

As they grew older, the boys partied more frequently and heavily, and it likely affected both their academics and extracurricular activities. By the time Tom reached senior year, he had dropped out of sports altogether. The personal inscriptions in their senior yearbook give a cogent look into the interests and personalities of Ricky and Tom. Ricky's favorite things were "rock and roll, guitars, summer, ganja" and his best memory was "Conservation Club trips." Tom reported his favorite things as "Blackfoot, Bob Seger, Wisconsin girls, fast cars" and his best memory as "getting an A+." Tom may not have earned his highest grade in his home economics class, but he made an impression on his teacher, who was quoted in the yearbook: "Tom was so intent on cooking that one time he forgot the dishwasher was running, and suddenly it overflowed!"

Tom's family life was not as carefree as his days at school. By the time Tom graduated high school, his parents had divorced and his mother remarried, to a man old enough to be Tom's grandfather. Later, several major events occurred in quick succession: Tom's father died, an infant nephew died unexpectedly, and Tom got married. He was not yet twenty two.

Tom's father was a welder in the shipbuilding industry, but he was known more for his drinking than his welding. The cause of his death was liver failure, the result of many years of excessive drinking. Like his father, Tom became a tradesman, working as both a residential and commercial electrician. Like his father, he became a heavy drinker. Tom's friends recognized his positive nature—he could be warm-hearted, fun-loving, and hilarious. But in the end, his life would be clouded by the dark effects of his drinking.

5

Trial Day Two

Day 2 began with jurors entering the courtroom at 9:08 a.m. They were welcomed by Judge Peter Diltz, who read them several pages of instructions about the case and the jury's role. Finally, it was time for opening statements.

After greeting the jurors and thanking them in advance for their service, prosecutor Tim Funnell launched into his presentation:

> On Christmas Eve 2001, the defendant Steve Owens stabbed to death Tom Azinger and did it with this sword [displaying it]. Mr. Azinger was taken by ambulance to Door County Memorial Hospital . . . from his mother's house where he had run after the incident. All life-saving efforts . . . were in vain and he bled to death . . . pronounced dead at 10:15 p.m.

Ms. Robinson interrupted: "I object. The use of material not yet admitted into evidence is not appropriate." She was referring to Funnell's displaying of the fatal sword.

Judge Diltz granted Robinson her point, partially: "Certainly, in the future you are right. It's discretionary . . . something we need to take up. You can continue, Mr. Funnell."

Next Funnell displayed an aerial photograph of the area that included Owens's apartment and Azinger's mother's house, 140 ft. away. Then he continued:

> Mr. Azinger and the defendant were friends for several years . . . Tom was invited . . . to a family

Christmas celebration but didn't feel right about going because he didn't have presents to bring.

Funnell then explained that Azinger arrived at Owens's apartment just as Greg Hoefman, Owens's roommate and Azinger's best friend, was preparing to leave for a family celebration of his own. Greg left shortly thereafter, leaving behind Azinger and Owens, both of whom appeared to be in good moods. The two men spent the next several hours talking, playing guitars, drinking, and smoking marijuana.

> Tom's mother returns home and almost immediately receives a call from her son. He states he is hungry and wonders if she could fix him something to eat. She had leftovers from the celebration and begins preparing them for her son. Approximately fourteen minutes later she hears a noise at her front door and thinks Tom may have forgotten his key, so she opens the door for him. Holding himself and bleeding, Tom stumbles in, saying he had been stabbed and telling his mother to call 911. She asks who stabbed him, and he replies "Steve." She helps him into the kitchen, where he collapses, bleeding heavily and having great difficulty breathing.

Funnell's dramatic beginning captured the jury's attention. He then spent considerable time describing the events in the apartment that led up to the stabbing. He quoted an interrogational report that Owens was very angry at the victim, due to a heated argument followed by a physical altercation that Owens was losing. The report, Funnell claimed, revealed no fear on Owens part. Yet, he forewarned, the defense would claim the defendant's actions were motivated by fear, thus entitling him to defend himself.

As he was wrapping up his opening statement, Funnell once again displayed the sword, this time removing it from its sheath. And once again Robinson objected. Diltz cleared the jury from the courtroom to confer with the attorneys. Robinson argued that displaying the sword was sensationalizing and inappropriate. Again Diltz equivocated: "It's discretionary with the Court—once you've shown it, I can't exclude it, but I don't disagree with you, Mrs. Robinson. . . . I will allow the sword."

The jury returned and Funnell finished his statement: "After all the evidence is in . . . I'll ask you to find the defendant, Steve Owens, guilty of first degree intentional homicide."

~ ~

Now it was Nila Robinson's turn. She outlined the critical issues relevant to her client's claim of self-defense.

> During the argument Owens went to the front door of the apartment and asked Azinger to leave. "Get out!" Azinger not only refused to leaved, he laughed at Steve. Owens then tried to walk away but was struck in the head from behind and placed in a strangle hold. Tom was larger and stronger than Steve. Only because Steve feared for his safety, possibly his life, he went to his bedroom and got his sword. When he returned to the living room, he pointed the sword toward Tom and again told him to leave. Tom leaned forward and reached for the sword, apparently trying to wrestle it away from Steve. It was at that point that he was stabbed. At the end of the trial, I believe the evidence will justify my request for a not guilty verdict.

Each attorney had spoken for about half an hour, Robinson slightly longer than Funnell. In all, the jurors had been listening for less than an hour and a half, but at 10:26 a.m. Judge Diltz offered them a morning break. Seventeen minutes later they were back to hear the first witness.

Over the next three days, the prosecutor would build his case with nearly two dozen witnesses. But to lead the way, he strategically chose first to call his most compelling one— Lorine Azinger, the victim's mother. During his opening statement, Funnell had already revealed the details of the victim stumbling into the arms of his mother, struggling for his life as she tried to save him. Now, Mrs. Azinger was about to express everything in her own words. The result was powerful, and heartbreaking. "Tom had been having a little trouble and had been living with me for about ten weeks," she began. Then she disclosed the events of the fateful day, beginning with the afternoon of December 24.

> I gave Tom a jacket for his Christmas gift. He tried it on and said, "This will be real warm, Mom. Thanks." Then I tried to get him to come with me to our family gathering that afternoon and evening, but he declined. When I left my house, Tom was getting readying to visit Greg and Steve. . . . [Five hours later, after returning home] I got a phone call from Tom, saying he was hungry, could I prepare him something to eat? I had plenty of leftovers from the family gathering, so I got two plates ready for him. A few minutes later I heard the front door rattling and assumed maybe Tom forgot his key. I went to the door to let him in and he just stumbled in.

At that very moment, Lorine Azinger's nightmare began— searing into her memory devastating images and sounds that would forever haunt her. She testified about her call to 911— how she struggled with the phone while trying to apply a towel to her son's profusely bleeding chest, as she was being instructed. Finally she heard emergency sirens arriving. It was a relief to turn her son over to capable hands, but he was lapsing into unconsciousness as the medics strapped him to a stretcher and rushed him to the ambulance. As Tom was being carried away, she feared she would never again see him alive. There was nothing left for her to do but telephone her other children and try to explain what had happened to their brother.

When Mrs. Azinger was excused from the witness stand, the jury might have extended a huge, collective sigh of relief. Her testimony had been emotional and exhausting. There was no rest, though, as prosecutor Funnell proceeded with a parade of witnesses, most of whom were law enforcement officers involved at the crime scene or medical professionals who tried to save Azinger's life.

~ ~

Wendy Allen was the first police officer on the scene. She described finding Azinger mortally wounded on the kitchen floor of his mother's house. After ambulances arrived and as paramedics tried to save Azinger's life, several other responding police officers turned their attention to the alleged crime scene, a mere 140 ft. to the west. The small, two-bedroom apartment was one of about twenty that comprised a five-building complex. Officers Carl Waterstreet Jr. and Tim Fuerst provided testimony about the crime scene.

Waterstreet was stationed outside the apartment, as Officers Fuerst, James Valley, and Gary Rabach prepared to enter. By training, the officers drew their weapons and readied themselves for an active crime scene. Were there other victims? Was the suspect still present? Cautiously they entered the front door, where they observed the front room in shambles, furniture demolished and a blood streak on a wall. It was a lot to take in. Fortunately, there were no other victims. The suspect was nowhere to be found.

While Waterstreet was outside of the apartment, he encountered Steve Owens walking up the street toward him. With pistols drawn, he and Officer Fuerst ordered Owens to lie face down on the ground and put his hands behind his back. Owens quickly obeyed, going to the ground. But before he put his hands behind his back, he raised them above his head and stated, "Go ahead and shoot me. I'm already dead." He was then handcuffed.

Waterstreet described transporting Owens to the downtown police station in his squad car. A dashboard camera recorded the two-minute ride, and the videotape was played in court. Owens was mostly incoherent, though there seemed to be a political element to his ranting.

Mark Witeck M.D. testified at length about the autopsy he conducted on Azinger. As Witeck narrated, Funnell showed the jury graphic color pictures of the victim's opened chest cavity, including the damage resulting from the sword blade that penetrated at least seven inches. The left lung was collapsed and the heart pierced. The death certificate identified the cause of death as "exsanguination [blood loss], due to sharp force injuries," whereas the manner of death was "homicide."

It was all enough to make anyone queasy, and several jury members turned their eyes away. When they did, they likely refocused on the victim's family members in the gallery. No one wore name tags, of course, but it was abundantly evident who was who. The grieving family looked stricken, horrified by the photos. It was a no-holds-barred approach by the prosecution. When jurors went home that evening, they would have a lot to think about, and the gory autopsy photos might even give them nightmares.

Judge Diltz decided to intervene. Maybe he felt the jury needed a break, maybe he himself was becoming overwhelmed, or maybe he had his eye on the clock—perhaps people were hungry. In any event, he dismissed court for a well-deserved lunch break.

After the break Dr. Witeck continued under direct examination. He described other, non-lethal injuries to the victim, including to the face, head, and back, presumably from the brawl with Owens. More significant were major cuts to both of the victim's hands—in fact, one of his fingers was nearly severed. These did not appear to be caused by a "defensive posture," that is, from hands held upward. Instead the victim apparently grabbed the sword blade with both hands.

Funnell provided a human skeleton so that Witeck could demonstrate that the sword entered the victim's chest at a 45-degree angle. On cross-examination, defense attorney Robinson scored a major point by getting the witness to admit that such an angle might have occurred if the victim had been crouching or leaning forward, or even lunging at Owens when he was stabbed. Robinson wanted the jury to consider that the two men had been grappling for the sword immediately prior to the fatal thrust. Finally Dr. Witeck's testimony came to a close. But if the jury assumed medical matters were over, they were mistaken.

Emergency staff from Door County Memorial Hospital testified about the frantic attempt to save Azinger's life. Emergency room physician Ken Johnson testified that Azinger had no pulse and was not breathing when he arrived at the hospital. Surgeon Kurt Scheer explained how he was called in to tend to the victim. He performed heart massage and sutured a large hole in the heart, all to no avail.

Tom Austad of the Sturgeon Bay Fire Department testified to being called to the crime scene to assist with emergency treatment. While standing in front of the Azinger house, he saw Owens walking up East Spruce Court in the direction of his apartment. Austad asked Owens what he was doing, and the reply was, "I suppose I'm going to meet the executioner." Funnell hoped the jury would connect the "executioner" comment with the "Go ahead, shoot me" testimony from Officer Waterstreet, thus indicating "consciousness of guilt" by the defendant.

~ ~

As Day 2 stretched into late afternoon, Greg Hoefman waited his turn to testify. For much of the day, he had been stuck in the holding room, where upcoming witnesses were isolated to prevent them from hearing anything that might alter their testimonies. Greg didn't handle boredom well, and he thought of a dozen places he would rather be. In fact, he didn't want to testify at all. His best friend had died on December 24, and Greg had arrived at the crime scene as Steve Owens, another close friend, was being handcuffed and hauled away in a squad car. Greg was prevented from entering his apartment that night, but the next day—Christmas Day—he returned to a completely different "home." No more Tom, and no more Steve, perhaps forever.

Now he was being called as a witness for the prosecution to testify against Steve. The door to the witness room opened and the bailiff called his name. His turn had come.

Q. How long did you know Tom Azinger?

A. Twenty-something years.

Greg explained the two had ridden the same school bus throughout grade school. After Tom graduated from parochial grade school and "came over" to Sevastopol High School in 1979, the two immediately became best friends. Over the years, their friendship never wavered. Were Tom and Steve friends? Funnell asked. "Yes." How long? "Six to eight years, maybe."

The questioning turned quickly to the afternoon of December 24. Greg slept late that day, arising in late morning to find Steve already up, sitting in his favorite chair, drinking coffee. The two spent the day at the apartment, except when "Steve went on a cigarette run." Tom arrived at the apartment later that afternoon, just as Greg was preparing to leave for his family's celebration.

Q. What were Tom and Steve doing in the few minutes before you left the apartment?

A. I can't remember for sure, probably playing guitars or video games.

Q. Were either injured, to your knowledge?

Trial Day 2

A. No.

Q. Either intoxicated?

A. No.

Q. Were they smoking marijuana?

A. No.

Q. Drinking?

A. Probably.

Q. Were they angry at each other?

A. No, quite the opposite. They were in pretty festive spirits, as it was Christmas. They were having a really good time.

Entered into evidence was a photo of a coffee table from the apartment, heavily littered with a variety of objects. A few spectators in the gallery exchanged glances, knowing fully that Greg and Steve put little effort into housekeeping.

Q. Describe what you see in the photo.

A. That table did get messed up a lot—it's nothing unusual.

Q. Can you identify the objects on the table?

A. A microphone, guitar magazines, a bottle, Pepsi can, controls for video games, a drum machine, a mug.

Q. What about those objects at the base of the bottle?

A. Looks like cigarettes butts, but that's not where they would naturally be. Usually they'd be in the ash tray.

Next Funnell showed a photo of the inside wall adjacent to the front door of the apartment. Hoefman identified three "chord charts," musical scales for the guitar. "Steve put them up." More critically, the prosecutor focused on a blood streak trailing downward from one of the charts. A final, dramatic question brought the direct examination to a close.

Q. Was that blood stain there when you left your apartment on the afternoon of December 24?

A. No, it wasn't.

Finally, it was Nila Robinson's turn to cross-examine the witness. Looking at the courtroom clock, though, she noted it was 4:58 p.m. "I prefer to cross-examine Mr. Hoefman tomorrow." Judge Diltz granted her request and dismissed the jury for the day. As he was leaving the witness stand, Greg Hoefman wondered if his time in court would ever end.

6

Humming and Strumming

Steve Owens and Tom Azinger could not wait to graduate from high school. Although Tom enjoyed his high school days more than Steve, commencement for both meant stepping into adulthood, with fewer rules and fewer authority figures. Or so they thought.

What to do with their free time, and what to do about earning money? Steve would have been happy to spend his newfound freedom by drawing, practicing his guitar, and taking nature walks. But he was still living at home and wanted to be independent. The best times of his young life had been flying, as well as crashing and repairing, the glider he shared with his friend Patrick. Now he wanted to fly for real! Steve's dad had spent his early adulthood in the US Air Force, and that sounded good enough for Steve. He enlisted shortly after his nineteenth birthday.

The air force was a good fit, a place to spread his wings. Instead of being surrounded by high school bullies and teachers who didn't understand him, he found himself among recruits just like himself. Importantly, none of them had ever met the old Steve Owens. They were willing to accept him as he was, quirks and all. Steve was ready to fly.

His hopes to become a pilot, however, did not materialize. Instead he was assigned to become a flight mechanic. Still, he enjoyed the work—the rigorous training, a full set of tools, and a seemingly unlimited budget for materials. All of it represented a huge promotion from his adolescent role as "chief mechanic" for the glider.

He got along well with his fellow airmen. Military life, on duty and off, promoted equal-status relationships, and his work buddies quickly became his friends. Everyone got nicknames—pointed, perhaps, but affectionate. "Thumbs" was the mechanic who was constantly dropping tools, "Straw" was extremely tall and thin, and "Glance" had a curious way of looking at everyone out of the corner of his left eye. Steve was nicknamed "Ozone."

Steve had an offbeat, stream-of-consciousness style of humor and expression, no doubt influenced by watching every episode of Monty Python with Patrick and other friends during adolescence. But his nickname had more to do with his interests and ideas, which were *way out there*—in the "ozone layer." He believed in certain things from the third dimension, such as remote viewing and astral projection, esoteric events his fellow airmen could neither understand nor refute. They may have viewed him as highly intelligent, or maybe simply "far out," but they liked and accepted him.

Steve managed to get along with his superiors as well, towing the line as necessary. But gradually Steve began to feel his officers were trying to trick him into disciplinary infractions. Whether true or not, things one day came to a head over a matter as small as a hat. While Steve was working on an airplane engine, a commanding officer appeared out of nowhere and ordered him to put his hat on. Under normal circumstances, the order might have been reasonable, but Steve was up to his elbows in grease and couldn't conceive of balancing a hat on his head while bending and straining to repair the engine. He refused the order.

It was a small act of defiance but enough to end his air force career. The discipline was three years' probation, with no chance of promotion. Instead, Steve chose to take an honorable discharge. At age twenty-four he found himself heading back home, once again a civilian.

~ ~

Patrick Jeanquart recalled the period when Steve Owens was in the air force:

Humming & Strumming

He seemed so well-adjusted to the military. We wrote letters back and forth and I thought everything was going great for him. When he came home on leave, he seemed perfectly normal. At some point, though, he told me some officers were trying to goad him into breaking the rules. That seemed a little odd to me. During that time his father's illness got worse and I think his family was pushing him to take a family medical dismissal, but he didn't.

After Steve got discharged, I rarely saw him, but he seemed to go downhill. I think he got into drinking and began talking about the occult. I wished he had stayed in the air force, because it seemed like the best thing for him.

Things did, in fact, go badly for Steve after his military discharge, and the decline was swift rather than gradual. According to Steve, "My best friend was killed in a motorcycle accident and I became very depressed. I said some things that I shouldn't have and was taken to [a psychiatric facility]." Admissions had no difficulty deciding that he met the criterion of "dangerous to himself or others" and readily admitted him on a voluntary basis for a seventy-two-hour observation.

After a hearing the facility kept him an additional twenty-eight days on involuntary status. He was diagnosed with paranoid schizophrenia and prescribed heavy doses of several antipsychotic drugs. After four weeks he was released but, in Steve's view, he was in worse shape than when admitted. The medications were producing some of the very symptoms they were supposed to relieve, and he felt terrible. Years later he took himself off the drugs "cold turkey," ending what he called "a seven-year coma." The diagnosis he received, however, would continue to plague him.

~ ~

Meanwhile Tom Azinger and Greg Hoefman were humming along in life after high school. An accomplished guitarist, Greg started a band and tried to make a living through music. He rounded up as many paying gigs as he could, typically in bars or at rowdy parties. Tom was in regular attendance and only partly because his best friend was playing. Tom loved loud, live music, and he loved to drink.

Tom tried not to let his partying interfere with work, and vice versa. If one took precedence it was partying, and part of partying was girls. His first girlfriend was Trenda*, a first cousin of Greg's. She, too, loved to party. More gregarious than Tom, she got along with everyone and could talk the leg off a stranger. But Tom and Trenda were only eighteen when they met, and their relationship was more casual and fun-loving than truly romantic.

Trenda wasn't ready to settle down and neither was Tom. That is, until he met Connie*. After a short engagement they were married in her church in Sturgeon Bay in 1986. He was just twenty and she was two years older. It is not clear what drew the newlyweds to Rawlins, Wyoming, but off they went. Growing up, Tom had rarely left his home state of Wisconsin. Neither had his best buddy and "best man," Greg Hoefman.

Shortly after Tom and his bride settled in Wyoming, he invited Greg out for a visit. Greg readily accepted and brought a friend along for company during the long drive. When Greg got twenty miles away, he stopped to call Tom for directions. Tom said it was too hard to explain—"just meet me at the 7/11" near a major intersection. Greg had no trouble finding the convenience store, but before he knew it, a local police officer pulled up, with squad car lights flashing. Greg was ordered out of his car: "Get down on the ground, face first, NOW!" *Did Wyoming police treat all visitors like this?* Next thing he knew, there was Tom, doubled over with laughter. It was all a big joke, designed by Tom in collaboration with a local cop he had befriended.

Humming & Strumming

The good times in Rawlins were relatively short-lived, though Tom's marriage with Connie would survive a few years, amid numerous battles. To the rescue came Trenda, Tom's old girlfriend. She moved to Wyoming and became part of the ongoing drama.

The following events occurred in Rawlins sometime within the general period of 1989–1992, their exact order and timing uncertain. Tom and Connie separated. Tom and Trenda began dating again. There were two separate allegations of domestic violence against Tom, one filed by Connie, another by Trenda. Tom spent a few days in jail. Trenda paid his fine, and after his release she and Tom moved back to Sturgeon Bay. One day after Connie's divorce from Tom was finalized, she married someone else.

Back in Sturgeon Bay, Tom and Trenda lived together for about two years, marrying at some point. It was a very stormy relationship, punctuated by calls to police. More than once Greg Hoefman interceded to pull his best friend off his cousin. But long after the relationship ended, Trenda refused to place all of the blame on Tom: "The violence was mutual. I'd go after him, he'd come at me. I can't say he was a violent person. It was more like he could be very aggressive when drinking, and that led to violence."

~ ~

When Steve Owens was released from the psychiatric facility after a month of treatment, he carried with him a bag full of psychiatric medications and a diagnosis of paranoid schizophrenia. Although his parents were supportive, Steve did not want to move back home, especially after spending several years in the air force and visiting cities like London and Amsterdam. He took a room above a rowdy bar in downtown Sturgeon Bay. It was a grim space—tiny and dark—but at least it was cheap, and with all the noise from the bar below, no one complained when he practiced his guitar into the wee hours of the night.

Fatal Sword

He hunted for a job and took the first one he could find. Washing dishes, and occasionally filling in as a short-order cook, was a far cry from repairing airplanes in the air force, but at least he was able to scrape by. The worst part was having to take orders from *everyone*, from owner down through head cooks and even servers. He bounced from one restaurant job to another. Then he hired on with Ricky Hoefman, Greg's brother, who ran his own commercial fishing tug. Hauling in fish from Lake Michigan was strenuous and cold work, but Steve got along great with Ricky and the crew. He recognized how dangerous the waters could be, so he followed the captain's orders explicitly. He trusted his friend to keep him safe.

Whether fishing or washing dishes, Steve never seemed to get ahead, and the heavy dosages of medication he was taking sometimes made it hard to function at all. He was always honest with potential employers, conceding his diagnosis of mental illness and the drug regimen he was on. When a job coach urged him to apply for disability, Steve agreed. He hated to consider himself disabled but was beginning to accept his apparent vocational fate—chances for suitable employment were bleak and might always be.

Steve began receiving monthly disability checks of about $500. It barely covered his living expenses but allowed him to work fewer hours, leaving more time to practice his guitar, hours and hours on end. He began appearing at "open mike" venues, where he would perform solo or with guest groups. He recalls once being "kidnapped" by a band that was particularly impressed with his strumming, and particularly desperate for a guitarist. "They kidnapped me! 'Get in our truck, we're taking you with us.' I said no way. They grabbed my guitar and said, 'Then we're taking your guitar, with or without you.' I had no choice so I jumped into their truck." Off everyone went, to another party where Steve performed with his captors.

Humming & Strumming

Soon Steve was playing regularly with a band called Zomar Blues. The group was reasonably successful, and his music earnings, along with his disability payments, enabled him to pay his bills and even buy an old car. His fellow musicians were a good bunch, and they generally tolerated his offbeat ideas and periodic rants about police and politics. Zomar was a good fit for Steve, but an unfortunate incident marred him for years.

Steve received a letter from an air force buddy. "Dear Ozone," it started. From a friend the nickname was a welcome sign of affection. However, a Zomar member happened to see the letter and excitedly began spreading the nickname to the entire band. To them, "Ozone" perfectly described the looniness of their guitar player. Even though Steve eventually left one band and joined another, the unfortunate moniker followed him. Worse, *everyone*, not just bandmates, began calling him Ozone, including acquaintances, police officers, and even strangers who might see him walking the streets of Sturgeon Bay. The nickname became a constant and cruel reminder of the psychiatric condition, or *diagnosis* at least, that continued to plague him.

A shared love for guitars first brought Steve and Greg Hoefman together. While Greg was in high school, Steve heard about the "fabulous guitarist from Sevastopol," but the two never met until Steve began playing with Zomar Blues. Greg's band was featured at a party in the country, and Greg let Zomar perform two songs. Steve's talent greatly impressed Greg. A couple of years later, when Greg's band Outcry needed a new guitarist, he invited Steve to join them. Steve was thrilled to accept.

Even Greg, who eventually became Steve's roommate and best friend, occasionally called him Ozone. But at other times Greg kindly tried to shield Steve from the nickname. Onstage, Greg would introduce Steve as "O'Jones," a deliberate attempt to stave off shouts of "Ozone!" from the audience. At other times Greg would go even further, introducing his favorite guitarist as *Doctor* O'Jones. This left some of Steve's tormentors with the perplexing notion that perhaps Steve possessed a doctorate in a field such as metaphysics. *No wonder we don't understand what he's saying!*

~ ~

After Tom Azinger's turbulent relationship with Trenda ended, the two parted ways but remained friends. "When I moved from Sturgeon Bay to Green Bay, Tom even helped me with the moving." The two rarely spent any time together after that, but because she was close to her cousin Greg Hoefman, Tom's best friend, she continued to hear all about her ex-husband.

After Tom and Trenda separated, they remained married for several years, even as each pursued new relationships. Tom dated Annie* for an undetermined period of time. Then came Candi*. When they began dating in approximately 1996, Tom was thirty-one and Candi twenty-five. After seven months of dating, they moved in together. An important part of the relationship, at least for Candi, was her two-year-old child from a previous marriage.

In about 1998, Tom and Candi became engaged. For two years prior, she had experienced Tom's violence, but only after he had been drinking heavily. But from 1998 on, she was constantly on guard against his outbursts, regardless of whether Tom was drinking. "It didn't matter [if he were drinking]. The slightest little thing, he'd snap. It happened all the time, but he was more violent when he drank. Then he'd *really* snap and take his anger out on me."

On two occasions Candi called the police to intervene. The first time, she had already fled the premises, so nothing was done. "The second time, *both of us* were arrested and taken to jail. After that, I stopped calling the police."

She sought help from the local domestic violence program and moved into an apartment to get away from Tom. She describes a classic depiction of abusive relationships: "He had this way of coming over, acting like a baby, swearing he loved me and would change. I loved him, so I'd go back." Would he change? "For about two weeks, then everything would go back to the nightmare."

~ ~

Were Tom Azinger and Steve Owens friends? A simple question, but the answer is complex. Steve met Greg Hoefman, Tom's lifelong friend, in 1986. Greg was a real extrovert, and to know him was to know his friends. When interrogated by police after the stabbing in 2001, Steve indicated that he had known Tom for fifteen years. But Tom married in the spring of 1986 and moved to Wyoming, so it is unlikely he and Steve became well acquainted until Tom returned to live in Sturgeon Bay in 1992.

Dean Cuyler* was a good example of how someone who knew Greg immediately became friends with his friends. Dean was dating Greg's sister Becki, and when Tom returned to Sturgeon Bay from Wyoming, Dean and Tom met through Gary and hit it off. Naturally Steve, as Greg's former bandmate and current roommate, became a friend as well.

Dean and Tom drank together and they worked together, for two different companies. In 1995, Dean and Becki moved to Green Bay, along with their infant. Shortly after, Dean asked Becki if Tom could come stay with them. Becki had known Tom since high school and always appreciated his fun-loving nature. He was friends with her brothers Ricky and Greg and she "saw him all the time, and at parties." So when Tom came to stay in her home, he was no stranger. At first things went smoothly.

Tom and Dean were working together in Green Bay but, as described by Becki, "Tom didn't have the best work habits," and it seemed to rub off on Dean. She was working hard outside the home and taking good care of her infant whenever she wasn't working. She expected the same of Dean, but Tom had different expectations. Things exploded one day when Becki came home and discovered her husband and Tom had neither worked that day *nor* taken care of the baby. Instead they had hired a babysitter and gone out to party. There was a big blowout, with nose-to-nose shouting. Tom was asked to leave immediately.

Eventually the relationship between Dean and Becki eroded and, in about 1998, Dean moved in with Greg and Steve Owens in their apartment on East Spruce Court. There he stayed for about six months, sleeping on the couch and using the large, unfinished basement whenever he needed extra room. Despite cramped quarters, the three seemed to get along well. Dean remembers, "Steve never liked conflict, so if things ever got a little tense, he just retreated to his room. Steve was pretty weird, but he was easy to get along with."

7

Trial Days 3 and 4

Wednesday, July 24, 8:47 a.m. Court was in session and Greg Hoefman was back on the hot seat. Public defender Nila Robinson began cross-examination by asking him to describe his friendship with Tom Azinger. Greg explained he and Tom had ridden the same school bus when they were little, became friends in high school, and had been very close ever since. Greg served as best man at Tom's wedding, and when Tom and his wife moved to Wyoming shortly thereafter, Greg drove out to visit them. When that marriage didn't work out, Tom returned to Sturgeon Bay and married Greg's first cousin Trenda. "Tom and Trenda had a trailer only about 50-60 feet from my place, so I saw them all the time."

Robinson then displayed photo exhibits of the living room of the Spruce Court apartment. Greg identified a broken picture on the floor and smashed furniture. He admitted he and Steve were not great housekeepers, but the living room was in reasonable condition and nothing was broken at the time he left on the afternoon of December 24. Wistfully, he identified a green recliner as "Steve's chair."

"Do you have an opinion regarding Tom Azinger's reputation for being violent?" Robinson's question got right to the heart of the defense's case—that Steve Owens feared Tom and acted out of self-defense. But before Greg could answer, prosecutor Tim Funnell objected, and Judge Diltz sustained the objection. Robinson requested a sidebar and the jury was cleared from the courtroom. Four minutes later Diltz called the jury back, and Hoefman was almost immediately dismissed from the witness stand. He had a feeling he would be called back.

Fatal Sword

~ ~

For the rest of the morning, the jury heard from six witnesses from the Wisconsin State Crime Laboratory. Fingerprints on the fatal sword were identified as being Tom Azinger's. Analysis of blood samples taken from both Tom and Steve indicated the presence of THC (marijuana), although the levels for both men were "pretty small . . . and not too different." Both men had blood alcohol levels consistent with intoxication, but it was not possible to determine accurately the levels at the time of the stabbing.

After lunch an Ameritech employee testified about phone records, which revealed that the phone call from the Owens apartment to Lorine Azinger's house began at 8:56 p.m. and lasted 10 minutes and 11 seconds. Presumably Tom and his mother engaged in casual conversation, probably about the family gathering.

Officer Dan Trelka of the Sturgeon Bay Police Department told about transferring Owens to the local hospital at 2:25 a.m. four hours after the stabbing. Owens appeared calm but was "rambling about the 9/11 attacks." Trelka attributed Owens's demeanor to both his emotion and intoxication.

Arleigh Porter described himself as a longtime officer for the Sturgeon Bay Police Department, in his third year as captain. He had taken fingerprints of both men and, on December 26, photographed injuries to Owens. More critically, he addressed the issue of why interrogations of Steve Owens were not videotaped, even though equipment was already set up in the interview room. For several minutes Nila Robinson grilled Porter.

Q. Was there a departmental policy against using audio and video in the interrogation room?

A. No.

Q. Was the equipment already in the room?

A. Yes.

Q. Why wasn't it in use then?

A. It was in use.

Q. Explain.

A. The equipment was used for monitoring the interrogation interview, not for recording it.

Q. What do you mean by "monitoring."

A. The interview was sent to a closed-circuit television in a separate room.

Q. For what purpose?

A. So that other officers could observe the interrogation.

Q. Why would they want to do that?

A. Possibly to pick up something the interviewer might miss.

Q. But wouldn't a videotape allow monitoring just as well?

A. It was against policy to videotape criminal defendants.

Next on the stand was Deputy Tim Johnson, K-9 officer for the Brown County Sheriff's Department. Johnson testified about being called to the crime scene to search for additional evidence. Actually it was the trained dog Toro that sniffed for clues. Johnson described leading the dog through the wooded area surrounding the apartment, searching for footprints and other evidence. Toro did indeed detect footprints in the snow but, more importantly, led officers to a "snow message" in the yard of the Bayview Apartments adjacent to the complex where Steve Owens lived.

Before Day 3 ended, three more Sturgeon Bay police officers took the stand. Deputy Jim Valley, one of the first officers on the scene following the 911 call, described his observations of the scene, including Owens's behavior.

Fatal Sword

Deputy Paul Keddell testified about Owens's demeanor as he arrived at the jail after his arrest. Owens was railing at the FBI and the 9/11 terrorists, but rather than being really angry Owens appeared agitated. Interestingly, Owens expressed that the local police were the "good guys." After about an hour Owens calmed down. Keddell did not recall Owens complaining about any injuries received in the fight with Azinger.

Officer Robert Osborne testified about observing the "snow message." Asked to state the contents of the message, Osborne tried his best but incorrectly substituted the word "thanks" at the end of the cryptic message. A court exhibit of a photo of the snow provided the actual wording and spelling: U DIE! I'M AREADY [sic] DEAD. ThAX X!

Judge Peter Diltz ended the day early, dismissing the jury at 3:53 p.m.

~ ~

Because of other duties of the judge and attorneys, Day 4 began late—at 11:00 a.m. It would be a short day for the jurors, who would only hear the testimony of four witnesses.

Carrie Gossen-Konrad was on duty on December 24 as a communications officer and dispatcher for the Sheriff's Department. Immediately after receiving the 911 call from Lorine Azinger, she dispatched police officers and emergency responders to the scene.

Guy Binish, an officer with the Sturgeon Bay Police Department, testified about photographing and videotaping every aspect of the crime scene. He also used his camera to capture the horrific aftermath within the home of Lorine Azinger.

Sergeant Gary Rabach of the Sturgeon Bay Police Department testified about being dispatched to the crime scene at 9:20 p.m. and arriving within a minute or two. At the Owens apartment he found the screen door closed but unlocked and the front door open three-fourths of the way.

50

Days 3 & 4

With weapons drawn, Rabach and another officer entered the apartment and immediately observed a "ninja sword type thing" on the floor close to the front door. He also testified there did not appear to be any nearby neighbors—potential witnesses—at home.

The lock to Steve Owens's bedroom was a simple thumb lock, plus it wasn't functioning properly, so it provided only privacy rather than safety. The door "could be opened with a good shove," Rabach explained.

~ ~

The next person to take the stand for the state might have been it's star witness, save for the victim's mother. He described himself as having more than twenty-six years experience with the Sheriff's Department, including the last three as Sergeant Investigator. It was he who interviewed Steve Owens at the police station on December 25, four hours after the stabbing, and again about twenty-eight hours later, on December 26. The investigator's name was Terry J. Vogel.

Prosecutor Funnell wanted to establish that no coercive techniques were used to get statements from the defendant. Vogel explained he had been formally trained to employ the Reid technique to interrogate criminal suspects. "I use a friendly, laid-back style to try to gain the confidence of the interviewee." The technique was superior to classic, outdated police tactics of harassing suspects, Vogel asserted. Avoiding harsh confrontation produces greater cooperation and thus more accurate statements.

Confident that Vogel had reassured the jury the defendant had not been browbeaten during the interrogation, prosecutor Funnell pivoted to the issue of the failure to videotape the interviews.

Q. Describe the interview room.

A. The room is very basic, 10 by 10 ft.

Q. And the video camera?

A. The camera was wired to a television set in another room, about 45 ft. away, where other officers could observe and be prepared to intervene, if the person gets unruly.

Q. Did the equipment have the ability to videotape?

A Yes, but it was not our procedure to do so.

Q. Describe your past interactions with the defendant.

A. I've talked to Steve Owens quite a few times in the past. We had a pretty good relationship.

Q. What was the defendant's demeanor during the first interview?

A. He was very angry at Tom Azinger. There was lots of profanity [addressed toward Tom]. Also, there was a fairly strong odor of alcohol on this breath.

Q. Did Owens ever express fear?

A. No.

The questioning of Vogel eventually focused on the actual three-page statement from the first interview. Vogel reported it took him an hour and a half to write the statement, which Owens "dictated to me."

The statement (see Source Document 3) was entered into evidence and projected in the courtroom. The prosecutor funnelled in especially on the final paragraph: "This statement was given of my own free will" and "I was read the Miranda rights . . . which I understood and agreed to waive."

Vogel pointed out that Owens signed each page of the statement, after having the opportunity to read and revise it. In fact, he did make a revision on page two, changing the phrase from "As I was stabbing him" to "As I stuck at him."

Days 3 & 4

By 3:37 p.m. the jury had been listening to Vogel for nearly two hours. Anticipating much more, Judge Diltz sent the jury out for a nine-minute break to stretch.

When court resumed Funnell returned to the issue of Owens's mood during the first interview with Vogel.

Q. Was he incoherent?

A. No. He rambled and I repeatedly had to get him back on track.

Q. Was he emotional?

A. Yes, very, very angry and hostile toward Tom Azinger.

Q. How angry did he appear to be?

A. I asked Steve to rate his anger on a 1–10 scale. He said, 'I'm a 10. I haven't been that mad in a long time.'

Q. Did the defendant express any fear for his life?

A. He didn't mention any.

Funnell then turned to the second interview of Owens, which began at 8:53 a.m. on December 26. (See Source Document 3.) At the outset of the interview, Vogel informed Owens that Tom Azinger had died as a result of the stab wound. Vogel testified that Owens seemed shocked, and bowed his head. In this interview, Vogel testified, Owens no longer swore at the victim and he became more defensive, claiming he had been scared and acted to protect himself and his home.

Maps drawn by Steve Owens, one during each of the interviews, were introduced into evidence. (See Source Documents 4 and 5.) In the second drawing Owens indicated where he had "stood [his] ground" immediately prior to the stabbing. Nearing the end of direct examination, Funnell asked Vogel if Owens had complained of injuries resulting from the fight with Azinger. Vogel testified that "no physical pain" was reported.

~ ~

The afternoon was growing late when Nila Robinson finally took the floor to cross-examine Vogel. There was a lot of ground to cover but not much time. She knew it wasn't ideal to split cross-examination over two days, but at least she would have the chance to bring out a few important points before the jury was dismissed for the day.

Robinson focused first on Vogel's contention that Owens changed his story from the first interview to the second. The implication during direct examination was that Owens, upon learning of Azinger's death, began to express fear, rather than anger, because he realized he could be charged with murder instead of disorderly conduct. Through her questioning, Robinson attempted to show that the fear was genuine, not manufactured to support a claim of self-defense.

In reality the discrepancies between the first and second statements seem superficial. For example, in his first statement Owens described the hold Azinger placed on him as a "headlock," in the second as a headlock *and* "chokehold." In the first statement Owens reported he and Tom had been in three other fights, the most recent about two or three years ago." In the second interview there no mention of fights. Was this because Owens was attempting to hide them, or because Vogel didn't ask about prior fighting? Robinson tried to establish that it was the *interrogator,* not the defendant, who was authoring the statements, that Vogel was summarizing the interviews rather than taking down Owens's words verbatim. Any discrepancies between the two statements might well reflect differences in Vogel's questioning, rather than Owens's demeanor or responses.

Perhaps Robinson had not ended as strongly as she had hoped. In any event, her time was up, and Judge Diltz dismissed the jury at 5:27 p.m.

8

Caregiver and Lifesaver

Steve Owens was a loner. Had it not been for playing in bands, and his friendship with Greg Hoefman, he might have been a recluse. But with one special family he connected in a way that revealed another side of him. It was a family that accepted him for who he was, "weirdness" and all. In return he provided loving childcare to their three children. He became more than just a friend—he was practically a family member himself.

Steve was only seventeen in 1978 when he first met the Rayniers, a young but growing family: Bob, age thirty; Cindy, twenty-four; and little Bobbi Jo, only four. Within months Bobbi Jo would have an infant sister, Deana, and seventeen months later, a little brother, Clint. The Rayniers lived on the north side of Sturgeon Bay, and Cindy had recently become good friends with Steve's sister Dawn, newly graduated from high school. It is not clear how the two met—very likely, during her high-school years Dawn had babysat Bobbi Jo.

The Rayniers were having a party and Dawn was invited. She brought along brother Steve, who remembers a lot of guitar music and drinking. Cindy liked Steve immediately. Bob was more cautious and slow to warm to newcomers. Over the years, though, Bob and Steve developed a close friendship few would have predicted. Steve was just trying to survive high school—a junior who didn't fit in and couldn't wait to escape. Nearly a generation older, Bob had been to Vietnam and back, not entirely in one piece. Combat shrapnel to his back resulted in a medical discharge and left him with a lifelong disability.

Over the next few years Steve had only irregular contact with the Rayniers. He served in the air force, was discharged, and then was slapped with the diagnosis of paranoid schizo-phrenia. By 1988, though, he had reconnected with the Raynier family.

Those intervening years had taken a toll on the Rayniers. Cindy and Bob were separated and heading toward divorce. Cindy was working two jobs—at a restaurant and driving a taxi—while trying to manage three children. Bobbi Jo had entered adolescence and was having difficulties, both during school and after. Sometimes Cindy knew where her daughter was, often she did not. Meanwhile, Deana and Clint, ages nine and seven, were a handful. Cindy needed help!

Steve Owens was willing to offer that help. He was en-tirely comfortable around children and already helped occa-sionally with his sister's young children, Ross, age four, and Logan, an infant. The Raynier household may have seemed chaotic to some, but to Steve it was a refuge from the outside world. That's not to say that babysitting several young ones was relaxing, but when it came to children, Steve had the patience of Job.

At any given time he might have been trying to track Bobbi Jo after school, dealing with Deana and Clint as they played wildly, and bustling to meet the needs of his two young nephews. Occasionally a neighbor left an additional child or two for a few hours.

Here is an incident that stands out in the memories of Steve, Cindy, and Deana, even decades later. Steve was changing Logan's diaper. All the essentials were laid out on the bedroom floor, Steve's preferred area for diaper-changing. Nearby was little Ross. From the living room came an out-burst involving Deana and Clint. Midway through the diaper change, Steve picked up Logan and dragged Ross along as he hurried to investigate.

A game of pocket billiards between Deana and Clint had escalated rapidly into a duel, with both kids brandishing cue sticks as swords, flailing at each other while on the run. Steve intervened, but with only two hands, he was hard pressed to referee while protecting his small nephews. In the chaos he himself suffered a couple of whacks before he could wrestle the pool cues away. Finally he established control and sat the two combatants on opposite ends of a nearby couch.

Calmly Steve tried to talk some sense into the youngsters. As he turned toward one end of the couch or the other to address the opposing Raynier children, tiny Logan's head swiveled from side to side. Nearby, Ross was wide-eyed.

"Pool sticks are for *pool,* not sword fighting. You could seriously hurt each other, put an eye out," Steve explained, even as a welt was appearing over his own right eye. He doubted his counsel was doing any good, but he had control of the swords and the children seemed contrite. At least temporarily.

Steve dealt with his little charges not so much by focusing on their behavior as by following a systematic plan of discipline, one that could have been lifted from a 1980s manual for behavioral parenting. Start at step one and go to the next level only as needed:

1. Take away Nintendo.

2. Unplug the television.

3. Take toys away and put them on high shelf.

4. Send kids to their rooms.

5. Stand them in a corner.

6. As a last resort, threaten: "If you can't behave any better than this, I'll *quit!*"

Steve's threat to quit was especially effective—the children were very attached to him and realized any replacement their mother could find would have been harsher and less fun. Today Deana remembers those early days: "Steve was very good to us. He was a different kind of character, but he was very kind and gentle. He wouldn't hurt a fly."

Fatal Sword

Cindy remembers Steve similarly: "He was the best baby-sitter *I* ever had. My kids were always clean and well cared for. He even tried to teach Bobbi Jo how to play the guitar. Steve would come over all the time, just to play cards, drink coffee, and be among friends. We'd all play poker, spades, cribbage, anything. And Steve loved to play cards with the kids and their friends."

~ ~

When Bob and Cindy Raynier divorced in 1989, they faced the potentially difficult decision of where the children would live, especially with Cindy's plans to move to Green Bay, an hour away. Fortunately everyone—parents and children—agreed: Bobbi Jo would go with Cindy while Deana and Clint would stay with Bob.

His marriage was over, but perhaps more devastating for Bob was his deteriorating medical condition. The aftermath of his war injury was syringomyelia, a chronic disorder that begins with a fluid-filled cyst within the spinal cord. The severity of the condition varies widely. In its mildest form, there is some discomfort that requires only monitoring, or perhaps surgery. In its most damaging form, syringomyelia causes severe pain, muscle weakness, and eventually paralysis.

When Steve met him in 1978, Bob walked with a limp. As his legs gradually gave out, he was forced to use a cane, then crutches, and finally a wheelchair. He adapted his van to accommodate his disability, but when his arms stopped working his driving days were over.

While Deana and Clint were growing older and more self-sufficient, Bob himself was becoming more disabled and less independent. The effects on his social life were also devastating. A gregarious person who enjoyed a wide circle of friends and social activities, Bob now found it difficult even to leave the house. He needed someone to help him watch Deana and

Caregiver & Lifesaver

Clint, and he also needed companionship. In stepped Steve Owens.

Steve and Bob had not always seen eye-to-eye. They varied in age by thirteen years and had different personalities. Steve was highly distrusting of government at all levels—federal, state, and local—and was particularly suspicious of local law enforcement, which he felt targeted and harassed him.

Bob, too, was distrustful of people, until he came to know them. But he loved his country and had answered the call when his government needed soldiers in Vietnam. It wasn't always easy for Bob to listen to Steve rail against the bigwigs in Washington and the military leaders who called all the shots. But Bob felt a kinship with Steve. He accepted what he had heard from everyone—Steve had schizophrenia. Steve's mental illness was as real as his own battle with syringomyelia, he felt. Neither disease was curable. Both men fought demons.

By 1999, Deana Raynier was twenty-one, her father Bob fifty-one, and they lived in the same residence. She was a single mother with a tot at her feet. But her father also needed full-time care, and Deana was happy to offer it, though it was a huge responsibility for a young adult. Her dad needed help with *everything*—bathing, dressing, tube-feeding, and toileting. Out of love she welcomed the duties. Still, at times Deana needed a break, if only for a few hours. That's when she called on Steve, who years before had babysat *her.*

Undoubtedly there was a degree of embarrassment involved when Steve began caring for Bob, trying to meet his proud friend's most basic needs. Bob quickly recognized in his friend a gentle, giving nature. Steve knew how to take care of Bob's physical needs, and he was sensitive to Bob's emotional needs as well. Whatever difficulties Steve may have had dealing with most people, he was calm and sensitive in the Raynier home. Bob knew he was in good hands.

Fatal Sword

Not many people are confronted with having to save a life, something most would prefer never to face. One afternoon such a predicament arose and hit Steve head-on as he was visiting Deana and Bob. Because of his tracheotomy Bob had periodic bouts of pneumonia, sometimes requiring hospitalization. On this occasion the pneumonia was back in full force. Without warning Bob's breathing became very irregular, a frightened look came over his face, and he fell unconscious. It was the moment Deana dreaded. She had played the scenario over in her mind many times, contemplating all the necessary actions. Still, she panicked.

Fortunately Steve stayed cool. Together he and Deana carried Bob outside to his van and loaded him into the backseat. Deana took the driver's seat while Steve stayed with Bob, trying to position him so he could breathe better. The hospital was only three minutes away, and Deana made it in record time. In the emergency room Bob stopped breathing. Deana thought for sure it was the end of the line for her dad, but the medical personnel thought otherwise. They were able to revive the patient, and within two days Bob was home, "good as new." Deana was grateful to the emergency room staff, but she credited *Steve* with saving her dad's life.

~ ~

In 1996, Steve Owens became roommates with Greg Hoefman. Steve needed a place to live and Greg needed someone to help him pay rent on his small, two-bedroom apartment at 7 East Spruce Court. The two had known each other for years. They shared a love of music and guitars, and in their younger years had played together in Greg's band Outcry and its successor Eight Miles High.

They were a good match. Steve valued privacy—more accurately, he shied away from most social situations not involving Greg. He could not shake the memories of those awful high-school years when he was constantly bullied. To him, almost anyone was a potential enemy. Greg, though, was a protector, not a bully, and Steve trusted him completely.

A sociable person who made friends easily, Greg was also a heavy drinker. He managed to stay on the good side of everyone—all he seemed to need to be happy was someone to talk to, or a drink in his hand. When Greg left his apartment, his destination was typically a bar or a friend's house. Sometimes he took Steve along.

For Greg, a special benefit of sharing his apartment with Steve was always having on hand a fellow guitarist to jam with. They converted the unfinished basement of their apartment into a concrete "studio," of sorts, undoubtedly rocking it with the reverberations from their dueling electric guitars. Just as importantly, Steve offered Greg a quiet, stable presence. It was not Steve's nature to pry into Greg's business or confront him about his drinking problems. Everything was in harmony—until a crisis arose.

When Greg had too much to drink, he often turned to the common strategy of "walking it off." In Greg's case, though, it backfired. Once he slipped on a steep hill behind his apartment and broke his leg. Another time he tripped on a step and fell on his head. Twice, Steve stepped in and did what was needed to get his friend medical treatment. Those two incidents, however, paled in comparison to the third.

Greg had been drinking heavily for several days. The more he drank, the more time he spent withdrawn in his room—for hours at a time. Steve watched on, hesitant to intervene. His roommate was an adult, and Steve wasn't a meddler. Still, he was quite concerned. Then Greg began to exhibit symptoms of alcohol poisoning. Steve could hear him vomiting repeatedly in his bedroom, and when Greg occasionally came out, he seemed lethargic and confused. His breathing was abnormal and a bluish tint appeared around his lips. Finally he began bleeding from the mouth.

It was a true medical emergency, and Steve responded accordingly. He called Greg's mother and explained the whole situation, then offered to find a way to get Greg to the hospital, or to call an ambulance. "No," said the mother, "I'll come get him. I'm on my way." She covered the usual twenty-four minute drive in only eighteen. Within a few seconds she realized Steve's assessment was correct—the situation was dire and Greg needed immediate treatment. Steve helped the mother get Greg into her car, and she rushed her son to the emergency room. Greg and his mother credit Steve with saving his life.

Following a few days stay in the hospital, Greg entered alcohol rehabilitation. Meanwhile Steve had the apartment to himself. He appreciated the solitude but missed his room-mate and worried about him. It was a long ten weeks until he got Greg back.

9

Trial Day 5

Day 5 opened at 8:48 a.m. with the return of Investigator Terry Vogel to the witness stand. Defender Nila Robinson continued to hammer away at the witness, pressing her contention that the written statements of Steve Owens during the jailhouse interviews were heavily skewed by Vogel's interpretations. Robinson particularly wanted to reveal how much Vogel knew about the stabbing prior to interrogating Owens.

Q. How much did you know about the events of December 24 when you interviewed Steve Owens early on December 25?

A. I knew Tom Azinger was dead, that a sword was involved in an argument, that there had been a struggle.

Q. Is that all you knew?

A. Well, I knew the victim stumbled from the apartment to his mother's house, and an ambulance was called to transfer him to the hospital.

Q. And Steve Owens had no idea that Mr. Azinger had died, correct?

A. At the first interview, no, I assume. But he knew at the beginning of the second interview, after I told him.

Q. Mr. Owens told you repeatedly that he should be able to defend himself in his own home. Correct?

A. Yes.

Q. That didn't make it into either statement, did it?

A. He didn't put it in his statements.

Q. He said it to you, correct?

A. Yes.

Q. And when you wrote those statements out, those words never made it into the account you prepared.

A. The account we prepared?

Q. Yes.

A. No, it did not. We did not have it in there.

Robinson hoped her point landed with the jury: Vogel had known all the relevant details *before* he started interrogating the suspect. But instead of building a framework from Owens's own statements, Vogel selectively used the defendant's words to bolster his own view of the fatal events. Specifically, and most significantly, Owens *did* bring up self-defense but Vogel failed to put it in the written statement.

The defense attorney also hoped her cross-examination successfully rebutted the state's claim that the defendant displayed "consciousness of guilt" in several ways—the snow message, remarks about "going to see the executioner," and daring the police to shoot him. But Vogel's testimony seemed to contradict the prosecution's claim. If Steve had no idea that Tom had been mortally wounded prior to the second interview on December 26, how could he have displayed consciousness of guilt on December 24?

Robinson had been questioning Vogel for eighty-three minutes, and Judge Diltz decided the jurors needed a morning break. After the recess Robinson completed her questioning and Vogel was dismissed from the stand. The court reporter herself must have been relieved. When the trial transcript was eventually completed, Vogel's contribution yielded nearly one hundred and forty pages.

~ ~

The name of the final witness for the prosecution was called. Typically when a new witness was announced, the jurors pivoted their attention to the door leading from the witness holding room. But when they heard the name "Thomas Baudhuin," they looked directly at the prosecution's table, where Baudhuin had been sitting as "second chair" throughout the trial.

Like most longtime city police officers, Baudhuin was very familiar with both Steve Owens and Tom Azinger, from patrolling the streets and from an occasional, generally innocuous police call. Interestingly Baudhuin lived in the same neighborhood as Steve's mother and maintained a cordial acquaintance with her. From time to time, as he drove past the Owens house, he had spotted Steve in the front yard, and Steve offered a simple, noncommittal wave.

Funnell took the witness through the various phases of the case. It seemed clear the two men knew each other well and had undoubtedly worked together on many cases. Baudhuin stated he was enjoying a pleasant Christmas Eve at home with his family when he was paged at 9:45 p.m. to respond to stabbing. At the scene he was advised by other officers of the details of the developing case. He entered the residence of Lorine Azinger and observed a large amount of blood on the floor in the kitchen and living room. At 11:45 p.m. Baudhuin met with Funnell in the district attorney's office to draft a "telephonic" search warrant. In a telephone call to Judge Diltz's home, Baudhuin read the warrant—several pages long—before the judge electronically signed it at 1:23 a.m.

Baudhuin then went to the lower level of the police station, where Steve Owens was being interrogated. He viewed the remainder of the interrogation from a nearby room, via closed-circuit television. After the interrogation concluded, Baudhuin met with Investigator Vogel to discuss the growing body of evidence about the deadly encounter.

At 3:50 a.m. Baudhuin returned to the crime scene and, with Officers Binish and Rabach, executed the search warrant, making a detailed list of objects found in every room. He was also present at 7:30 a.m. when the canine unit arrived from Green Bay, and he helped direct Toro, the dog, to the proper area to sniff things out. Hours later Baudhuin drove the sword—the suspected murder weapon—to a state crime lab in Wausau. The next day Baudhuin attended the autopsy of Tom Azinger in Green Bay.

In short, prosecutor Funnell could ask for no better witness than Baudhuin to conclude his presentation of the state's evidence. By directing the witness through his various observations, activities, and reports, Funnell was essentially providing the jury a closing summary of his case, even before the defense began calling witnesses of its own.

Defender Nila Robinson faced a dilemma. Cross-examining the witness would allow the prosecution to bolster its points through re-direct. On the other hand, failing to challenge Baudhuin might give the jury the impression that his testimony was impeccable. She did her best.

Robinson was able to establish that, while Baudhuin did observe portions of both interviews of Owens, he was not present in their entirety because of other duties. Yes, he admitted, his own perceptions of Owens's demeanor might have been influenced by what he had already learned from other officers on the case. Mostly though, she chose to focus on the issue of the perplexing decision at the police station *not* to videotape the interrogations of Owens.

Baudhuin explained the protocol, as other prior witnesses had: The police department was committed to videotaping interviews of victims of assault, including minors who had been sexually assaulted, but not criminal defendants. The equipment was always in place in the interview room, but not all officers had the expertise, or authority, to videotape interviews. Yes, Baudhuin admitted, the equipment was readily available, but only to provide a closed-circuit feed to the observation room.

After a volley of re-directs and re-crosses between Funnell and Robinson, Baudhuin was excused from the witness stand and returned to his place at the prosecution table. Then Funnell informed the court: "The state rests its case."

10

Defense

The prosecution had laid all its cards on the table. To them, it was a straight flush. The victim and the defendant, after drinking heavily for several hours, engaged in a heated argument, mostly over terrorism. The defendant ordered the victim from his apartment, but the victim refused. Verbal fencing turned into fisticuffs—a real brawl. Realizing he was losing, the defendant rushed to his bedroom and returned to the living room with a 38-inch sword. He roared at the victim once more to leave the apartment, but the victim merely laughed at him. Outraged, the defendant fatally stabbed the victim.

The defense team had to show that the victim's death was a tragic accident, rather than the result of a deliberate act. Steve Owens was only trying to defend himself in his own apartment, as he is legally allowed to do. After being assaulted Owens was motivated by fear, not anger, and he made several requests—warnings—to the victim: "Get out of here!"

The effectiveness of the defense's case hinged heavily upon showing that Tom Azinger, when drinking, was an aggressive person, and that Owens, having known Azinger for years, was well aware of his aggressive nature. He had certainly heard of Tom's propensity for violence and had himself fought with Tom on two prior occasions.

Would defense attorney Nila Robinson be allowed to call the witnesses to testify that Tom became verbally and physically aggressive when drinking? At a pretrial hearing in April, Robinson stated her intention to introduce evidence not only of Azinger's *reputation* for violence but also *specific acts* of

Defense

violent conduct that were known to Owens. At that hearing, Robinson claimed there were 5–10 such acts currently "under investigation." Judge Peter Diltz expressed concern about the potential effect of such an investigation on Owens's memory. As any such acts were discovered, Owens would obviously be made aware of them—it was, after all, an investigation conducted by the defense *for him*. This newly acquired information could affect his pending testimony. District Attorney Tim Funnell seconded Diltz's concern, adding that if Owens had access to police reports, he could simply read them and incorporate the prior acts into his memory.

As a matter of style, Judge Diltz liked to keep his trials moving at a reasonable pace, and at the trial's outset he had informed the jury to expect the trial to last only 7–8 days. Now Day 5 was coming to a close, and the defense had not yet begun its case. Robinson was asking to lead a procession of witnesses to the stand to show that Azinger was an argumentative person who could become verbally and physically aggressive when he drank. Funnell would surely cross-examine each witness at length and might even call rebuttal witnesses. Furthermore Diltz feared the testimony in aggregate would amount to nothing less than character assassination, shifting the entire focus from the actions of the defendant to the character of the victim.

After considerable wrangling outside the jury's presence, Diltz finally decided the matter. He would allow Robinson to call 5–7 "reputational witnesses." Her total time limit would be approximately thirty minutes, partly to keep things moving and partly to limit the "cumulativeness" of testimony. And any questioning about "specific acts" would be barred. Robinson realized that the judge's decisions would make it far more difficult to effectively defend her client.

~ ~

Nila Robinson would have preferred to begin calling her witnesses at the outset of a new day, when the jury was fresh, or at least following lunch. But the breaks did not fall her way. All morning the jury had been listening to testimony from Vogel and Baudhuin. At least Judge Diltz allowed a brief morning break before Robinson began.

The first witness for the defense was Gary Smith, Robinson's longtime private investigator. In fact, he was more than just a PI. Over several years he had worked closely with Robinson on dozens of criminal cases. And at present he, like Thomas Baudhuin, was serving as "second chair" for his side.

A few weeks after the stabbing, Smith had interviewed numerous potential witnesses for the defense. He was not permitted to testify in court about those interviews, but Robinson did question him about his observations when he took a "field trip" to the police station. The goal of that visit was to study the room where Owens had been interrogated, as well as the nearby room where officers watched on closed-circuit television.

Smith described the physical characteristics of the rooms but, more importantly, testified about the presence of the videotape equipment and his interactions with the local police. Yes, the video equipment was still present, even months following the interrogations of Owens. The equipment seemed to be a standard part of the interrogation room, rather than routinely moved about.

Q. Did you ask if interrogations were systematically videotaped?

A. I was told, "not for criminal suspects."

Q. Would the equipment be difficult for most people to use, with minimal training?

A. It would not be challenging.

Q. How much would a videotape cost?

A. About two dollars.

Defense

Robinson knew, of course, it was her client on trial, not the Sturgeon Bay Police Department, but she hoped the jury would appreciate two critical points. First, the absence of a videotape of the interrogations deprived the jurors of the opportunity to evaluate for themselves Owens's demeanor during the two interrogations. Second, there was no way to determine if the statements of Owens—written in longhand by Investigator Vogel—accurately reflected the interviews in their entirety.

~ ~

Robinson was now ready to call six witnesses to testify that the victim was known to be a violent person. People in the court gallery came to attention, anticipating these witnesses would be widely known in their community. How would *they* describe Tom Azinger?

First to testify was Trenda Rios*, the second wife of the victim. She explained that she and Tom had dated and broken up, each gotten married and divorced, then dated each other again. Finally they married but stayed together only about two years. After they separated in about 1991, they continued to see each other occasionally as friends, both before and after their divorce in 1998.

Defender Robinson realized she would have limited time to question each of her witnesses, so she cut to the chase.

Q. Do you have an opinion as to Mr. Azinger's character for violence?

A. He had a reputation for being violent.

Q. Was that your personal opinion as well?

A. Yes.

Prosecutor Funnell's cross-examination consisted of only one question:

Q. Were you at the Owens apartment at any time during December 24, 2001?

A. I was not.

Next was Gwen Marsh, a bartender at a popular drinking spot in town at the time. Gwen was nervous about testifying and spoke a little too fast, apologizing, "I never had to do this before."

Robinson asked her the name of her place of employment. Her answer was rushed and not entirely clear, and Funnell interrupted to apologize for not understanding her answer. Judge Diltz clarified things: "She works at the Neighborhood Pub. I eat lunch there all the time." Under further questioning Marsh explained she had worked at the Pub for ten years and had known Azinger as a customer for most of that time.

Q: Do you have an opinion as to his character for violence?

A: He was very, very outspoken . . . I don't want to say bad, but always—I don't want to say—looking for an argument - - always had an opinion about everything.

Q: Do you have an opinion as to whether he was violent?

A: I think he sure could be and I have seen him interact with customers.

Robinson tried to probe a little further. "This is an area in which I cannot ask you about specific instances." At the mention of "specific instances," Funnell objected and asked for a sidebar. Moments later the judge excused the witness.

If there were any doubt about her discomfort at testifying, Marsh dispelled it by announcing *I'm out of here!* as she scurried from the witness stand. Funnell then moved to strike her testimony and Diltz agreed, informing the jury:

Defense

"You are to disregard the witness's testimony and not consider it in any way in reaching your verdict."

Jane Hoefman*, the mother of Greg Hoefman, was next to take the stand. Her son had known Tom Azinger since the boys were in high school. "He went with both of my boys," meaning her other son Ricky was also a friend of Tom's.

> Q. Would Tom Azinger come to your home sometimes?
>
> A. He was out there a few times. Kids would have parties and things.
>
> Q: Did you know Steve Owens?
>
> A. I do.
>
> Q. Were you familiar with other people who knew Tom, in addition to Greg and Ricky?
>
> A. He was married to my niece Trenda.
>
> Q. Did you know other people who were acquainted with Tom?
>
> A. Sure.
>
> Q. As a result of your familiarity with him or with that community, do you have an opinion about his reputation for violence?
>
> A. Yeah, he had a reputation. He got violent.

Again Funnell's cross-examination was brief and to the point. He asked the witness if she had seen either Azinger or Owens on December 24, and the witness admitted she had not.

Next was Becki Hoefman*, Greg's sister and Trenda's first cousin. She explained she knew Tom Azinger because of these family connections and because she had attended high school with Tom.

Q. Was there a time when Tom lived with you?

A. Yes . . . during January and February of 1996.

Becki further explained that Tom was her friend but moved in only because of his close friendship with her boyfriend Dean, who also lived at her apartment.

Q. Do you have an opinion as to Tom's reputation for violence?

A. Yes, he's violent.

Funnell's cross-examination was again short and simple, as he confirmed that the witness had seen neither Azinger nor Owens on December 24.

The fifth "reputational witness" was then called to the stand. Annie explained she had been Tom's girlfriend for roughly three years, until about 1995 or 1996. They had lived together, first in Sturgeon Bay and then for about a month in Georgia. When the relationship ended she returned to Sturgeon Bay alone, with Tom later returning.

Q. Did you work for a time at the Greystone Castle [a popular bar in Sturgeon Bay]?

A. Yes.

Q. By virtue of where you worked, did you see Mr. Azinger out socially, with other people?

A. Mostly by himself.

Q. As a result of that familiarity with Mr. Azinger, do you have an opinion about his reputation for violence?

A. No, I don't. What we had was anything but a normal relationship.

Defense

Q. Do you personally have an opinion about whether or not he is violent?

A. I don't think he really was, not to me.

The witness's answers to the last two questions caught Robinson completely off-guard. Though Funnell, too, was probably surprised—the answers seemed too good to be true—by habit he asked the witness if she had seen Azinger or Owens on December 24. Of course she hadn't.

Robinson had an opportunity to re-direct the witness:

Q. You had an interview with Mr. Smith sometime ago, correct?

A. Somebody, yes, yes.

Judge Diltz interrupted, calling for a sidebar. Then he dismissed the witness. If Robinson had been hoping to impeach Annie's testimony based on a prior sworn statement, she was thwarted.

The last witness of the day was Michael Woldt. He explained that he ran a business called Woldt's Corner Bar and from time to time would see Azinger at the bar.

Q. Did you sometimes see him interact with other people?

A. Yes.

Q. As a result of that familiarity, do you have an opinion as to whether Mr. Azinger was a violent person?

A. No.

Q. Do you have an opinion about whether he had a reputation for being a violent person?

A. Personal opinion?

Q. Yes.

A. Yes.

Q. And what is your opinion?

Before Woldt could answer, Funnell objected, and Diltz invited Robinson to ask further "foundational questions." Robinson proceeded to establish that Azinger was a patron of Woldt's bar, that the witness knew other people who knew Azinger, including Tom's girlfriend Candi, who worked employee at his bar. Again Robinson asked the key question.

Q. Based on your familiarity with Mr. Azinger, do you have an opinion as to whether he was a violent character?

A. I have never seen him being violent but [in my opinion] he is.

On cross-examination Funnell asked whether Woldt had personally seen Mr. Azinger be violent. Woldt answered he had not, but Tom's girlfriend used to come to work with "bruises from him." It wasn't Funnell's preferred answer, so he pivoted quickly and established again that Woldt had never *personally* seen Azinger be violent and that Candi might have "gotten the bruises anywhere."

After a few more questions from both attorneys, Judge Diltz dismissed the witness by thanking him for testifying. Woldt responded with an informal *Yup.*

Robinson told the court her next witness would be Steve Owens, and she preferred not to call him to the stand at the end of the day. Judge Diltz agreed, telling the jury: "It's been a long week, so I'm going to let you go at 4:45 instead of 5:15." After delivering the usual admonition not to discuss the trial with anyone, not to avail themselves of news reports, etc., he dismissed the jurors for the weekend.

11

Flying

By 1993, Steve Owens found himself in a personal fog. For nearly a decade his life had gone nowhere—a discharge from the air force, his father's declining health and death, dead-end jobs, and failed relationships with girlfriends. Perhaps most devastating was the realization that his dream to become a professional musician was over. What did he have to show for the past ten years? Only the constantly annoying nickname Ozone, it seemed.

He blamed most of his problems on the "system"—the collection of all those privileged, self-centered, and corrupted individuals who seemed to conspire against him. Now it was time to take control of his life, instead of letting others determine his destiny. The first step was to break free of the psychotropic medications he had relied on for years. Although the drugs occasionally seemed to smooth out his thoughts and emotions, generally they made him feel dull and lethargic, unable to function. Getting off the meds was the first step to making big changes in his life.

First he stopped the medications cold turkey—against medical advice and without supervision. It was rough going for several weeks but he was determined. Next he moved from his small place in a rooming house to the rambling farm of his friend Carl Whitford. Agrarian life was a godsend. Any time of day or night, he could chop wood or wield a sledge hammer, look for wildlife, or tend his garden. Once more he could see the open sky, which reminded him of the best parts of his childhood, going to the nature preserve in Milwaukee and, later, flying the glider with his pal Patrick.

Fatal Sword

Steve stayed at his rural home for two winters. By the spring of 1995, he felt like a new person. Ready for fresh adventures he packed up his camping gear and hitched a ride to Nashville, Tennessee. Soon he found work on a construction crew, where he was assigned to the high beams, performing minor repairs and painting. It was the best-paying job he ever held, but the most terrifying as well. While his fellow workers walked confidently across the beams, Steve put safety before pride and *scooted.*

A kind boss named Skip helped him overcome his fear of falling, by starting low. " There was a beam lying on the ground, and Skipper told me to hop on it and start walking. I did what he said but it seemed silly—'It's a lot easier walking down here than way up there!' But he convinced me it was all the same, then showed me how to carry my tools to maintain balance. He was good teacher and the best boss I ever had."

After a few months the construction job ended. Tennessee had been a good experience but he was ready to head back to Sturgeon Bay. Walking the beams, high in the sky, made him yearn again for flying. His mind kept returning to thoughts of his junior-high ventures with the glider. Though he had rarely reached heights of even ten or fifteen feet before landing hard or crashing, gliding was a thrill he could never forget. Now he dreamed of flying for real, soaring higher and farther than ever. His new horizon would be clear and bright.

First, he would obtain his pilot's license. Then he might pursue commercial piloting, which would earn him enough to attract a wife and provide for a family. He would prove to all of his detractors that he *could* succeed. His mother, sister, and nephews would be proud of him. Flying lessons would be costly and time-consuming, he knew, but he was up to the task.

Steve got a job at the Cherryland Airport, close to Sturgeon Bay, helping with the routine tasks of running a small

Flying

airport. More importantly he talked to pilots whenever he got the chance. Some of them loaned him instructional manuals, and Steve saved every penny of earnings for private lessons. He completely abstained from alcohol and drugs in any form and poured over flight manuals. He was inching his way toward the cockpit.

At last he hired a flight instructor, Wes, and took to the skies. The initial lessons went great, with pilot and student quickly developing a rapport. Cognizant of Steve's limited resources, Wes even invited him to rent the upstairs in his family home in Algoma—a way to justify charging Steve reduced fees for lessons. For Steve, Wes's house was more than a nice place to live. It was a new *home*—offering acceptance, and a step toward a normal life.

As training continued Steve displayed a real aptitude for flying. Finally he was ready to fly solo, his pilot's license within reach. Then one day, in mid-flight with Steve at the controls, Wes dropped the bomb that Steve secretly feared. "You know, Steve, the FAA knows about your mental diagnosis. It's only a matter of time until they ground you." Steve could only nod, as he tried to hold back tears of anger. In silence the two completed the flight. After landing, Steve was distraught and began to vent, expressing frustration toward a system that branded him with an inaccurate diagnosis and continued to damn him years after his symptoms were gone.

Wes tried to calm him. "Steve, you know I think you could be a great pilot, or I would never go up in the air with you. And if I thought you were a freak, you wouldn't be living upstairs in my home, with my family." It was of little consolation for Steve, who realized his flying days were over. At least in Door County.

~ ~

A few weeks later Steve loaded his 1985 Chevy Cavalier with all of his earthly possessions, including camping gear. He couldn't wait to make Wisconsin disappear in his rearview mirror. He said goodbye to Wes in Algoma, then headed north to Sturgeon Bay, where he bid farewell to his mother and to Bob Raynier. As miserable as Steve's own life seemed, seeing his friend confined to a wheelchair provided a sad reminder of misfortune in other forms.

Then he began driving. The plan was not to stop until he reached Prescott, Arizona, or his car broke down—whichever happened first. Hour by hour he drove on, stopping only for gas, sandwiches, and snacks. After 1200 miles and 24 hours of driving, he alerted suddenly to find himself driving off the road. Somehow he managed to bring his car to a halt just short of a ditch.

Where was he, and what time was it? A road sign indicated he was in Texas, and he didn't need a watch to tell him it was time to crawl into the backseat for a nap. Three hours later he emerged from a deep sleep to marvel at the new day. The sun was rising and he had only 700 miles to go. The Cavalier was holding up, and so was he. Just one final stretch to his journey's end, and a new future, he hoped.

Steve arrived in Prescott in the middle of the night, dog-tired. He could do little but find a vacant parking lot and spend another night in his car. Waking at sunrise he thought he was dreaming—the surroundings were so beautiful, the mountains inspiring and the horizon unending. Maybe this was the "tomorrow" he had been seeking since his discharge from the air force so long ago. He fueled his car, checked the oil, asked for directions, and set out for his future.

Steve's destination was Prescott Municipal Airport (Earnest A. Love Field). Though he knew the general direction of the airport, eight miles north, he quickly spotted planes in the sky and let them guide him home. Without enough money even to rent a room, let alone pay for flying lessons, finding a job came first. His four years experience as an air force mechanic, along with his recent job at Cherryland Airport, would make him a shoe-in for employment, he

Flying

hoped. And he knew Love Field was home to Embry-Riddle Aeronautical University, a privately-run flight training school.

Luckily the airport was hiring. After completing an application, he was instructed to find Bruce Jaeger in a nearby office. The name rang a bell, and not because it called to mind the famous Chuck Yeager, an air force pilot who gained fame by breaking the sound barrier in 1947. *Bruce Jaeger,* Steve thought, trying to place the name. When he got near Jaeger's office, he heard the man's familiar voice, and when he shook Bruce's hand, Jaeger exclaimed, "I know you!"

Jaeger had been an air force recruiter in Door County in 1980, when he spoke to Steve Owens about joining the armed forces. Fresh out of high school, Steve enlisted, and his four years in the air force, despite a rocky ending, were the best years of his life. Now he stood before Jaeger again, hoping for a new start, perhaps the next best years of his life. After some reminiscing and a brief interview, Jaeger hired him.

Steve readily adapted to his new duties, such as fueling planes and maintaining the tarmac. He basked in the fresh, western air of Arizona, and he loved the open beauty of the surrounding mountains. After two weeks on the job, Steve was beginning to view his new life as a "mile-high experience," matching the elevation of Prescott, and so far removed from his troubled life in Wisconsin.

Steve was getting along great with his coworkers, who liked him and treated him with friendliness and respect. When a substantial snow fell in late February, shortly after he began at the airport, they teased him about bringing a "Wisconsin blizzard" with him. His break room was near a small but comfortable office, and he became work friends with Jen*, a long-time employee several years older than Steve. She seemed protective of him, like a big sister. It was to Jen that Steve first shared his goal of taking flying lessons, once he had saved enough money.

Fatal Sword

One warm spring day Steve was clearing brush from a fence line surrounding the tarmac. He stepped on a mound of fire ants and immediately sustained bites on both legs. He tried to brush the ants away, but they were ferocious, biting his hands as well. Steve headed straight for Jen's office.

"I've been attacked!" he shouted.

"Attacked? By whom?" Jen responded.

"By a thousand little bastards! Fire ants!"

"Go to the bathroom and wash with cold water and plenty of soap," Jen directed. She sounded like she knew what she was talking about, so he obeyed. When he returned Jen had him cover the stings with moist towelettes. As he was sitting there recovering, Jen put two fingers to her eyes and then touched them to her computer screen. When Steve seemed puzzled, she repeated the gesture and quickly left the room.

Catching on, Steve moved to Jen's chair and looked at the screen. There was his personnel file. Beside the routine information such as his birth date and social security number, he saw: Psychiatric diagnosis—schizophrenia. It was only a phrase, but it destroyed his Arizona dream. *So stupid! I should never have given them my real identification.*

His past had followed him westward, and his aspirations had been destroyed once again by the omnipotent Federal Aviation Administration (FAA). He cursed the psychiatrist who labeled him, then cursed himself for believing the diagnosis and accepting the prescribed treatment. He couldn't bring himself to curse his father, years dead by now, though Steve knew the critical role his dad's trusting nature had played in it all. "Do what the doctors say. They know best."

Steve worked another ten days at the airport, just to earn enough to put his newest disappointment behind him. Watching new students shake hands with their flight instructors was too much to bear. Though he didn't blame Jen for his misery—he was grateful to her, in a way—he couldn't bring himself to stop by her office for a final goodbye.

Flying

Should he leave the United States behind? Head for Canada or South America, where the FAA could no longer track him and ruin his life? It was tempting, but Door County was where he had spent most of his life, where his mother was living. He had an open invitation to live with his best friend Greg Hoefman, and he would be near the Raynier family, who would always accept him.

On the long drive back to Wisconsin, Steve seethed at his misfortune in life, how a single psychiatric diagnosis, years before, could ruin his life. *Screw the FAA.* He vowed to fly without their approval, on his own terms. He would build his own glider and fly it whenever and wherever he wanted.

He scrimped and saved for a year before he could begin to purchase parts for the glider. It would take another year to complete construction and make his creation flightworthy. By spring of 1999, he was ready for the initial flight. He thought of his old friend Pat, his first "co-pilot" from glider days of long ago. Steve would have liked a little ceremony, but he was alone. Maybe that's what "flying solo" meant, he thought.

Over the next two years Steve flew his glider every chance he had, two or three times per week, if weather was favorable. He amassed hundreds of hours of flight, and gliding was the best thing—about the only thing—he had going for him. Early each October, though, when fall began giving way to the cold Wisconsin winter, Steve would put his beloved glider in storage. He always felt sad but reminded himself that spring was only six months away. He couldn't know in October 2001 what life-changing events were around the corner.

12

Building Up

The disastrous clash between Tom Azinger and Steve Owens on Christmas Eve 2001 was, seemingly, spontaneous and unpredictable. A series of events in each of their lives, however, left them both reeling, and vulnerable. For Tom, the downward spiral started months earlier. For Steve, years earlier.

~ ~

On April 4, 2001, Tom Azinger's girlfriend filed for a temporary restraining order on the grounds of domestic abuse. Details are not clear. Possibly another explosive incident had occurred or, instead, after years of alleged abuse Candi finally decide enough was enough. Either way, she made the decision to part ways with her boyfriend of five years. At a hearing on April 9, Judge Peter Diltz granted an injunction, with a firearm restriction. In effect the court said to Tom Azinger: Surrender any firearms you own or possess, and *stay away from Candi.*

~ ~

On May 28, 1998, Steve Owens was involved in a two-car accident near the highway bridge in Sturgeon Bay. It was a Thursday evening and traffic was heavy, with tourists flowing into Door County for a weekend of rest and relaxation. For out-of-towners and locals alike, Highway 42 is a main thoroughfare. A long, arching drawbridge spans the junction of two large bodies of water—Lake Michigan and Green Bay. On the southern run-up to the bridge is a roadside shoulder, but on the bridge itself the shoulder disappears. The speed limit is 45 MPH but on that day in May, traffic was moving much slower.

Approaching the bridge from the south, Steve found himself in a long line of vehicles. Directly ahead of him a semi-trailer truck blocked his view of oncoming traffic. Directly behind was a car with at least four occupants, including a driver growing increasingly impatient with the slowdown. *His* travel agenda was apparently much more urgent than those of other drivers. He couldn't pass on the left, due to oncoming traffic, so he tried to take Steve's vehicle on the right, using the shoulder to pass before attempting to butt his way back in.

Steve had other ideas. "He was on my right, trying to force me left, into oncoming traffic. I could have been killed! I did the only thing I could do, I bumped his car before he hit mine." The bump landed the passing car in a ditch, and Steve drove on. "I sure wasn't going to stop and see if the jerks were okay. They would have beaten me to death." To Steve it was a harrowing incident, though he escaped without personal consequence.

Not so fast! Eleven days later Thomas Baudhuin of the Sturgeon Bay Police Department issued Owens a warrant, citing him for reckless driving (traffic offense) and, more seriously, hit-and-run (traffic misdemeanor). Steve decided to fight the charges, due partly to righteous indignation and partly to impoverishment. He appeared in court on June 15 to plead not guilty to both charges.

The more serious charge resulted in a jury trial, and on November 18, 1998, he was found guilty and sentenced to one year probation and twenty-five hours of community service. The reckless driving case dragged on for months. Finally on March 1, 1999, he pled "no contest" and was fined $147.50. Steve could not, or would not, pay it, so his license was suspended.

Like many people whose driving privileges have been suspended, Steve continued to drive. On December 2, 2000, he was caught, cited by Officer Greg Zager for driving with a suspended license. Instead of fighting the charge, he pled "no contest" and was fined $150.50. Once again, he did not pay, so his license was suspended a second time. To the court system Owens was little more than another troublemaker caught in a revolving door. To Steve the charge was yet another case of being harassed by the local police. With few exceptions he disliked and distrusted most of the local police force. As far as he was concerned, they had painted a target on his back years ago and continued to hound him. Even in the worst situation, he could not fathom calling the police for help.

~ ~

Greg Hoefman had a lot of friends. When they felt like partying, they were drawn to Greg like a giant magnet. He could put together a golf outing in minutes. Tom Azinger and Steve Owens were sure bets, and Greg easily rounded up others to join in. The gatherings were always great fun, and good golfing had little to do with it.

When Greg invited friends to his apartment, the atmosphere was free-and-easy. Everyone knew the basic rules: Bring your own guitar and bring your own intoxicants. Friends who partied at Greg's knew they could count on Owens—Ozone—being around. Maybe he would join in, or maybe he would stay in his room. But it was Greg's apartment, they felt, not Steve's, even though the two had been longtime roommates.

In late summer of 2001, one particular gathering began in typical fashion but took a bizarre twist, and relationships would be severely tested. There were five at the party: Greg, his brother Ricky, Ricky's girlfriend Mary Beth*, Tom, and of course Steve. Naturally there was guitar playing but the main focus seemed to be on drinking and drugs, certainly marijuana and perhaps pills as well. Likely it was not a matter of *who* would become intoxicated but *when* and to what degree.

Ricky fell asleep, or unconscious, on the couch. Greg left the living room to spend some time in either the bathroom or the basement. Tom and Mary Beth, hand-in-hand, entered Greg's bedroom and shut the door behind them. Sensing trouble, Steve reacted in his characteristic manner—he headed to his bedroom and closed himself in, escaping the dicey situation.

When Greg returned to the living room, he was puzzled to find no one there, except Ricky. He went to his bedroom door and peaked in. "What the hell is going on!" he yelled. The outburst roused Ricky, who groggily realized something bad was going on and sensed he was the victim. Exactly what was occurring in the bedroom varies according to who tells the story. In one version the hanky panky involved a sexual encounter between Tom and Mary Beth, right under Ricky's sleeping nose. Ricky exploded. Hostilities quickly turned physical on the front lawn. Inexplicably Ricky chose to pummel his brother, not Tom.

Why attack Greg instead of Tom? Maybe Ricky felt everything was Greg's fault, since it was his brother's apartment and party. On the other hand, Tom was a formidable foe—larger and more experienced in fighting than Ricky, or Greg for that matter. Regardless, while the brothers Hoefman were in combat, Tom chose to slink away, unscathed.

There is a second, less damning version. In this one, when Greg opened his bedroom he found Tom and Mary Beth smoking *his* marijuana. He was outraged they would do so without asking permission. When Ricky was startled by Greg's shout of "What the hell?" he assumed, incorrectly, that Tom and Mary Beth were dallying instead of smoking. And he suspected that Greg had instigated the bedroom escapade, perhaps with a wisecrack that turned into a dare.

Which version is closer to the truth? Regardless, Ricky's reaction was unambiguous. After attacking his brother,

Ricky threatened to do the same to Tom the next time they met. He also demanded Greg ban Tom from the apartment. The length of the ban, and whether it was enforced, is unclear.

~ ~

What was the exact date of the fiasco at Greg's apartment? Likely it was on or about Labor Day, September 3, 2001—perhaps a few weeks earlier. In any event, Tom and girlfriend Candi had a huge argument on Tuesday, September 4, with the earlier catastrophe at Greg's apartment likely playing a contributing role.

Tom came to the door of Candi's apartment and knocked loudly. After spending years with Tom, she knew instinctively he had been drinking and trouble lay ahead, so she pretended not to be home. When he finally left she sought refuge at the nearby house of her friend Angie. But Tom returned and headed straight to Angie's to confront Candi. "He fought with me and started to cry. Things were getting out of hand—there were several other people there, including kids—so I went into a back bedroom and hid. Tom left but came back about five minutes later. He was swearing, hurt and angry. 'Tell me it's goodbye, Candi, tell me it's over.' So I said, 'Goodbye, Tom.'"

It was not the answer Tom wanted. He left and soon saw Steve Owens on a bike. He asked Steve to join him for drinks at a nearby bar, and Steve accepted. No doubt Steve got an earful of Tom's grievances against Candi. Within minutes Tom argued heatedly with other patrons. The bartender intervened and kicked Tom out of the bar. Steve was welcome to stay, and he did.

According to Candi, Tom returned to her apartment and there was an ugly confrontation in the parking lot. He pleaded for her to give him another chance—"one last time." She refused and Tom threatened her: "You're going to die!" Then he tried to hit her with his car. She fled into her apartment, then heard a loud BAM! "I looked out the window and he had hit my car. He backed off of it and took off like a bat out of hell. I came out to inspect the damage but luckily there wasn't any. Someone else in the complex called the police."

Tom was arrested by Sturgeon Bay police and charged with four offenses: disorderly conduct, driving while intoxicated (3rd offense), criminal damage to property, and knowingly violating a domestic abuse order. Three days later he appeared in front of Judge Peter Diltz for a bail hearing. Cash bond was set at $1000 and Tom was ordered: to have no contact with Candi, not to operate a motor vehicle without a valid license, and to maintain absolute sobriety. No one stepped forward to pay the bail, so Tom remained in jail. There he sat when news came of the 9/11 terrorist attacks on the nation.

On September 14, Tom again appeared before Judge Diltz. Remarkably Candi asked that the restraining order, imposed just a week before, be lifted! Tom remained in jail three more days—a total of thirteen days—until his mother finally posted the $1000 cash bond.

In exchange for a place to live, his mother no doubt imposed certain rules and conditions. Tom was thirty-six years old and in no mood to be living like a teenager with his mother. He had little choice. Out of steady work and without driving privileges, he was cash poor, to put it mildly. His devious, if not outrageous, behavior at Greg Hoefman's party had strained his long friendships with Ricky and Greg, as well. Worst of all, he wanted Candi back, but she wouldn't have him.

In earlier times Tom's closest friends affectionately nicknamed him "Tommy Zoom," due to his constant quest for fun and excitement. Tom didn't care much for the "Tommy" part—it seemed too informal—but he relished the "Zoom." He liked fast times and friends who could keep up. As 2001 was drawing to close, however, his life had fallen apart. He had lost his longtime girlfriend, his job, and the privilege of driving a car, *any* car at *any* speed. The twinkle in his eyes had faded, and Tommy had lost his zoom.

~ ~

In a different way, 2001 was a dispiriting year for Steve Owens as well. Instead of the dire straits Tom Azinger faced, though, Steve faced longstanding problems with no easy solutions. The best time of his life—his tour in the air force—was long past. His ambition of becoming a professional musician was over, one failed band after another. First it was Zomar, then Outcry. Outcry broke apart and morphed into Eight Miles High but, in Steve's words, that band went "six feet under." Finally he tried to lead his own bands—Psy-Metrix, followed by Jet Lag. Neither really got off the ground.

Similarly, Steve's dream of becoming a pilot was over. When the FAA intervened, its purpose was to prevent a seemingly unstable person from piloting a plane. To Steve, though, it was the end of his vision for success in life. There could be no well-paying career that might attract a spouse and lead to a family of his own. The future seemed dismal—stuck in Greg's small apartment, endless hours practicing the guitar, drawing, and tinkering with his chemistry set. Was this all that was left in his life?

13

Trial Day 6

D-Day had arrived for defendant Steve Owens. His trial had not proceeded as he hoped but, pessimist that he was, he was not surprised. He had wanted a change of venue. A jury of Sturgeon Bay citizens, in his view, would be deferential to local police and thus primed to judge an eccentric like himself very harshly. On Day 1, his fears began to be confirmed as the jurors were selected. Most of them seemed familiar with the police officers scheduled to testify and favorably impressed with prosecutor Tim Funnell.

Things didn't get much better on Day 2, when Funnell's opening statement appeared far more effective than that of his own attorney. Then he sat through days of testimony by police officers, especially Baudhuin and Vogel, who seemed to him to be twisting the truth. Finally, when his attorney took the floor, she seemed handcuffed by the judge's rulings, especially when testimony about "specific acts of violence" was blocked. But now on Day 6, Owens would have the opportunity to state his case. He had to convince the jury his fatal actions on December 24, 2001, stemmed not from anger but from self-preservation, a fear for his own life.

The jurors were escorted into the courtroom at 8:57 a.m. eager to hear the defendant's version of Christmas Eve. How would Owens characterize his friendship with the victim? How would the defendant describe the events leading up to the showdown with Tom Azinger? What actually precipitated the argument and what, if anything, did Owens do to try to deescalate the situation? But above all was the question of motive. When Owens moved from the living room to his bedroom to get his sword, what was he feeling? Fear for his life, or anger?

After Owens took the witness stand and was sworn in, defense attorney Nila Robinson did not beat around the bush. She asked him two critical questions.

Q. Did you intend to kill Tom Azinger?

A. No, I did not.

Q. When you left your apartment that day, did you have any idea he was mortally wounded?

A. No, I did not.

Next Robinson tried to rebut the prosecution's contention that Owens had displayed "consciousness of guilt" by writing the "snow message," stating he was "going to see the executioner," and challenging the police to shoot him.

Q. When you left your house that day, did you know whether or not Mr. Azinger was bleeding?

A. He must have been, the way he grabbed the sword.

Q. You heard [testimony] that you were crying out, "Shoot me, just shoot me." . . . Did you say that?

A. Probably, because I couldn't figure out what the big fuss was.

Q. When you walked up the hill [toward your apartment], what did you expect the police were going to do?

A. I don't know. Question me. "Hey, Steve, we want to talk to you about this."

Q. When you were placed under arrest, what were you told was the offense?

A. Disorderly conduct, I think I was told.

Q. Did anyone tell you Tom was seriously injured?

Trial Day 6

A. No, nothing about it.

Q. In terms of how you were feeling, the events of the night, how did you feel about it at the time?

A. Drunk, tired, just sick.

Q. You heard Officer Waterstreet testify about your rambling about Osama bin Laden, the 9/11 attacks, and things?

A. Yes.

Q. Did you do that?

A. Probably, yes. I would think so.

Q. Any idea what led you to go on about Osama bin Laden in the backseat of the squad car?

A. It's what started our whole argument that evening.

Q. You've been described as raging against Tom Azinger that evening. Were you doing that?

A. Yes.

Q. Were you using bad language?

A. Yes. I was wondering why they didn't arrest him too.

Q. Were you angry at Tom?

A. Yes, I was. He should have been arrested so I was asking where he was.

Q. Are you talking about the scene, the squad car, or the jail?

A. The jail. I was expecting them to pull him in there too. I kept peeking out of my cell, yelling "Where the hell is Tom?"

Q. Did anyone tell you Tom was seriously injured or dying?

A. No, they didn't.

Robinson was ready to move on to the interrogations conducted by Investigator Terry Vogel.

> Q. How did it come about that you had a conversation with Sgt. Vogel?
>
> A. He came to my cell and asked, "Do you want to talk about tonight?" and I said, "Yeah, sure" because I didn't have nothing to hide.
>
> Q. Did you want to talk to the police?
>
> A. Yes, I did.
>
> Q. Why?
>
> A. To tell them what happened.
>
> Q. Let me be blunt. Did you want Tom to get into trouble?
>
> A. Yes, I did. I didn't see why I should be the one in trouble about this whole incident.
>
> Q. Did you feel it was fair that you were the only one arrested?
>
> A. No.
>
> Q. Did you talk freely to Sgt. Vogel?
>
> A. Yes. I didn't think I was going to get into much trouble.
>
> Q. Did anyone accuse you of battery . . . hurting another person?
>
> A. No.
>
> Q. Only thing you heard was disorderly conduct?
>
> A. Yes.
>
> Q. Do you think you had been disorderly?
>
> A. No, not really. I just wanted Tom to leave.
>
> Q. Did you tell that to Sgt. Vogel?

A. Yes.

Q. Were you asked any questions that you weren't willing to answer?

A. No. I answered all his questions.

Q. Did you ever tell him you were scared [at the apartment]?

A. I believe I did. I don't remember him writing it, though.

Robinson wanted the jury to hear her client's version of what happened in the apartment on December 24.

Q. What happened when Tom arrived at your apartment?

A. I said, "Welcome in, Tom." We said "Merry Christmas" to each other. He had his guitar and his duffel bag, and he said, "Do you want to jam?" I said, "Sure." Tom was having trouble with the bridge of his guitar and asked me to fix it. In the meantime Tom picked up Greg's bass guitar and began to play it."

Robinson asked Owens about how the argument began.

Q. Did you have the television on?

A. Yes, it was on most of the day. I set it on the TV Guide station, with the sound way down, just let it run, like I always did. Moving background, I guess.

Q. The TV Guide was on the whole time?

A. Yes.

Q. What images are on the Guide?

A. The channels and what's on. At the top they show images or clips, with little captions.

Q. Did something of significance come on?

A. Yeah, two smoking buildings.

Q. The 9/11 attack?

A. Yeah.

Q. Before that, you guys had got along? No problems?

A. Yeah, no problems that I could detect.

Q. How much of the brandy had you consumed to this point.

A. Pretty close to all of it.

Q. Back to the 9/11 attacks on television, did that start a conversation?

A. I told Tom what everybody should know. The CIA got their spies out there, FBI, somebody had to know something. And he said, "We should go and nuke all of them." I thought that was absurd.

Q. You had different opinions about what should be done?

A. He thought we should nuke them all. I said we should find the ones responsible. Otherwise we'd have more problems, just lobbing nukes around. Big problems. He didn't seem to think so.

Q. How long did the argument go on?

A. I don't really know.

Q. Then what happened?

A. He went to the kitchen to use the phone.

Q. When Tom returned, what did the two of you do?

A. He sat back on the couch and didn't seem in too good a mood, I don't know why.

Q. Was his mood connected to you in any way?

A. I had no clue.

Q. Did he pack up his guitar?

A. He said he was going to leave in a little while. I said, "Yeah, all right. I'll probably be leaving soon, too."

Q. Then a fight got going?

A. Yeah.

Q. How did it start?

A. I'm really not sure what started it. Something about me getting my Social Security checks and having it made. I just didn't want to hear no more about that, and the 9/11 stuff, and I wanted everything to be mellow and quiet.

Q. He said you had it made because you got $6000 a year from the government?

A. Yeah, something like that.

Q. Had it reached the point where you were saying insulting things to him, also?

A. Yes, but I don't remember what about.

Q. How did you feel about Tom complaining about your getting $6000 a year?

A. I didn't like it too much. I'd about had it. I wanted him to leave and told him, "Tom, just leave now." I really had enough being insulted.

Q. Were you cussing each other?

A. Yeah, something like, "Get the hell out." Something to that effect.

Q. As you were walking [away], tell me about the first physical contact.

A. I felt a blow over my right shoulder, it could have been a forearm.

Q. Could it have been something else?

A. No, I don't think so.

Q. Then what happened?

A. I kind of stumbled and caught myself.

What about the history of fighting between them? Robinson wanted Owens to tell the jury in his own words.

Q. Have you and Tom been in some physical fights before?

A. Yes.

Q. How many?

A. Twice, I think.

Q. How did they start?

A. Arguing.

Q. How did they become physical?

A. He'd grab me. One time it was at the apartment, about two years ago. Greg broke it up.

Q. The other time?

A. At Sunset Park.

Q. Your statement [to police] indicated there was a third fight, or was that wrong?

A. That was wrong. I was thinking a total of three fights [including December 24].

Q. Did you get hurt in those fights?

A. I didn't come out ahead.

Q. Did you have any injuries that sent you to the hospital?

A. No, no.

Q. Did you experience physical pain in the prior fights?

A. Yes.

Q. Did you win?

A. I lost.

Q. How would the fights end?

A. The one by the park, I kind of cried "uncle." The other one, Greg broke up.

Q. So that one didn't get very far?

A. No, it got as far as him slamming me against the wall.

Robinson asked about Tom's putting him in a headlock on December 24, and Steve demonstrated the hold on himself, remarking "my neck hurt, tweaked." He also testified that Tom had effectively used the chokehold in previous fights.

Q. How much did you weigh last December 24?

A. About 142 pounds, kind of a light guy. . . . I'm up to 181 lbs. after being in jail.

Q. Did you report neck pain at the time?

A. That night, no, because it was kind of numb . . . later, yes, it still kind of bothers me.

Q. Did you have a prior neck injury?

A. Yeah, I wrecked a hang glider when I was fifteen and tweaked my neck, and it's bothered me off and on ever since. But not on December 24. It was kind of mellowed out.

Q. Back to the fight, you were on the ground, wrestling the chokehold. How did you get away?

A. I don't know.

Q. What did Tom do?

A. I thought he reached for something.

Q. Reached for what?

A. I don't know, I wasn't going to wait around to find out.

Q. As you moved away, what was your intention?

A. To get a weapon.

Q. Why?

A. I just wanted this to stop and didn't know any other way to do it.

Q. Did you think you could win a physical fight?

A. No, I couldn't.

Q. Did it occur to you to find the [cordless] phone and call 9-1-1?

A. I didn't know where it was and didn't have time to look. Everything happened fast and furious.

Q. Were there other rooms you could go to?

A. Yes, but I didn't want to get cornered.

Q. Did it occur to you to go out the back door?

A. No, it didn't. Anyways, to get out the back door you have to move the telescope, the garbage can, the recycling bin, other things, and the [door] lock is kind of weird.

Q. When you went to get the weapon, what was your intention?

A. To scare him away. I was serious about him leaving.

Q. At the time, you actually had two swords, right?

A. Yes, I did.

Q. Why did you pick this one?

A. It was closer. I knew exactly where it was.

Trial Day 6

Robinson asked Owens to rise from the witness stand and demonstrate for the jury the pose he used to confront Azinger.

Q. That stance you just now showed us . . . is that just some idea you came up with, you learned somewhere?

A. Just a defensive position. I got my arm up with the least amount of blade possible. I didn't want to endanger either one of us. I didn't want to get thrashed around anymore either.

Q. This sword has been referred to as a "Samurai sword." Is there something about it that makes it a Samurai sword?

A. Just the way it's made, I guess. I don't know.

Q. What's your opinion about what a "Samurai" is?

A. I don't know. Chinese warrior. Guard. I don't know.

Q. You said there was about four feet between your body and Tom's?

A. Yes.

Q. What did Tom do when you assumed your stance?

A. He laughed at me.

Q. Did you think he was taking you seriously?

A. No.

Q. What did he do in terms of moving toward you?

A. He crouched down, like a boxer, and came towards me.

Robinson instructed Owens to return to the witness stand.

Q. Did you say anything to him at this point?

A. I think I made it clear that, you know, he had to go.

Q. Did you actually say that?

A. Yes, I kept saying that. I don't know how many times I told him he had to leave.

Q. One of the statements that Sgt. Vogel wrote, that you said something to Tom about "Get out or I'm going to stick you."

A. Yeah, that was probably the last thing I said to him.

Q. If Mr. Azinger had been willing to leave, what was your intention then?

A. Let him go. I wasn't keeping him a prisoner.

Q. What happened next?

A. He grabbed the tip of the sword, the end of the blade.

Q. He had one hand on the sword, or two?

A. He had his left hand on it, and his right hand over his left hand like he was trying to wrestle it away from me. That's exactly what it felt like, too.

Q. Did he pull the blade toward you?

A. Well, he was trying to pull it away from me, back toward him.

Q. What did you do?

A. I - - - I poked him with it.

Q. Why did you do that?

A. To get him away from me. There's no telling what would have happened if he got it away from me, which he was trying to do.

Q. Even at that point, did you intend to kill him?

Trial Day 6

A. No, I didn't. That's when I kind of got scared . . . really scared.

Q. When you held a weapon and told him to get out, did you expect that he would?

A. Yeah, I figured he would. I think anyone would.

Q. You know a sharp sword can hurt someone?

A. Yes, I know that.

Q. You were willing for that to happen?

A. No, I didn't want it to happen, but I didn't know what else to do.

Q. Sitting here now, can you think of any really good alternative to what you chose to do that day?

A. No, except be elsewhere earlier.

Q. When you jabbed at him, did you know whether or not the sword entered his body?

A. No, I did not. I thought it might have caught his shirt or still be in his hands.

Robinson then shifted to the circumstances in which Owens gave a second statement to Vogel on December 26.

Q. How did it happen that you talked to the police again?

A. They came to me and asked if I wanted to talk again, and I said yes. They wanted more detail about what happened.

Q. Were you given some Miranda rights about whether or not you had to do this?

A. Yes. I waived them.

Q. Were you given more information before that interview?

A. That Tom had passed away.

Fatal Sword

Q. Who told you that.

A. I think it was Captain Arleigh Porter.

Q. How did you feel when you heard Tom died?

A. I didn't feel good about it. At first I didn't believe it. I thought it was some kind of sick joke.

Q. How did you find out it wasn't?

A. They were insistent, said they weren't kidding.

Q. Did you understand what caused his death?

A. I figured it had to do with the altercation.

Q. Did they tell you about Tom's wounds?

A. They told me it was the result of a sword wound in the chest area.

Robinson then went back to the moment of the stabbing. Owens reaffirmed that he had no intention of hurting Tom, but he had tried everything. In the end he had no choice.

~ ~

It was Tim Funnell's turn to cross-examine the defendant. He felt he had already scored all the points he needed through four days of his witnesses. Still, Funnell was itching for the chance to sharpen his case, and he went on attack.

Q. How long have you owned that sword?

A. A year or two, I'm not exactly sure.

Q. I'm showing you Exhibit 80. Is this the sword we're talking about?

A. Yes.

Q. And this is the scabbard you bought along with it?

A. Yes.

Trial Day 6

Q. Would you agree with me that this sword is designed to be a weapon?

A. Yes.

Q. A lethal weapon?

A. Yes.

Q. It's sole purpose is to inflict harm, correct?

A. Yes. Well, it's a showpiece too.

Q. Well, you didn't have this up on a wall, did you?

A. No.

Q. Or in a display case . . .

A. No.

Q. . . . so that people could see it but not get hurt?

A. Well, I was going to eventually.

Funnell continued, emphasizing that rather than displaying the sword as a showpiece, Owens chose to keep the sword in his room. Owens explained the sword's primary purpose: he leaned it against the curtains next to his bed, to keep the sunlight out while he slept.

Q. I'd like to talk about this sheath for a second. It was on the sword when you went to your bedroom?

A. Yes.

Q. You took the sword out of it?

A. That's correct.

With a flourish Funnell drew the sword from the sheath and asked Owens if that's how he had done it. "I don't know if I used that exact motion," Owens responded. Funnell then asked Judge Diltz for permission to hand the sheath over to the jury. Diltz asked Robinson if she had any objection, and she didn't. After the jurors got a good look, Funnell proceeded.

Q. Mr. Owens, you ever swung a baseball bat?

A. Yes. Many times.

Q. You agree this sheath is very hard plastic?

A. Yes.

Q. When you took the sheath off the sword, you made a conscious decision to use the sword and not the sheath, right?

A. I wanted to scare him away from me.

Q. Well, you could have taken the sheath off of it, could have confronted Tom. See how I'm standing, like a baseball player?

As the jurors watched Funnell assume his slugger's stance, they may have recalled when, only fifteen years earlier, Funnell had been a star baseball player for the local high school. Funnell continued.

Q. "Tom, get out of here or I'm going to nail you over the head with this." You chose not to say that?

A. Because I didn't figure it would work.

Q. Holding an object like a baseball bat, with the ability to clock someone over the head, wouldn't be sufficient?

A. No, I didn't have any intention of clocking or sticking anybody.

Funnell then addressed the friendship between Tom and Steve. The defendant agreed that, though they had fought twice before, he never really had serious problems with him.

Trial Day 6

Q. You had no problem with Tom coming to your house on December 24?

A. No.

Q. No problem getting drunk with him?

A. No.

Q. No problem smoking marijuana with him?

A. No.

Q. No problem getting into an argument with him?

A. I didn't want an argument with him, much less anything else, Mr. Funnell.

Q. When the argument began, you could have just left, gone to your mother's, without arguing with him. You could have just said nothing, right?

A. Saying nothing to Tom *is* an argument.

Q. You could have agreed with him.

A. I tried to agree with him.

Q. Just for the sake of having him shut up and get out, you could have said, "Yeah, you're right."

A. I've had enough arguments with Tom to know if you agree with him to avoid an argument, he'll complain you don't mean it and keep on arguing.

Eventually, cross-examination came to a close, followed by an exchange of re-directs and re-crosses, before Owens was finally dismissed from the witness stand at 2:00 p.m. He had been on the hot seat for five hours.

~ ~

The next witness for the defense was Tom's longtime girl-friend, Candi. As she explained, the two had been together, off and on, for a period of six years, though there had been frequent breakups, amounting to "two weeks here, a month

107

there, and so on." Their final parting occurred about ten weeks before Tom's death.

Judge Diltz's prior ruling disallowing testimony about "specific acts of violence" left little room for questioning by defender Nila Robinson, so she focused on one critical question.

Q. Did Tom Azinger have the capacity for violence?

A. Oh, yes. He was very violent.

Next to the stand was Dean Cuyler. He testified he had been close friends with Tom for ten years, and a close acquaintance of Steve's for about three years.

Q. Did Tom have a capacity for violence?

A. Depending. . . when we were just hanging out, he could be a super guy. But if he was drinking . . . violence is a word you could use.

For the third time, Greg Hoefman was called to the stand, this time as a witness for the defense.

Q. How long have you known Tom Azinger?

A. For twenty-five years. Tom was a very close friend.

Q. And how long have you known Steve Owens?

A. Also about twenty-five years.

Q. Did Tom have a reputation for violence?

A. Yes.

The defense was done. The prosecution took advantage of its privilege of rebuttal testimony, and prosecutor Funnell called four witnesses. His goal seemed to be to show that the failure to videotape the interrogation of Steve Owens was due merely to departmental procedure. There was no deliberate attempt to conceal anything.

The most notable of the rebuttal witnesses was Investigator Connie Schuster, Door County Sheriff's Office. She described the videotaping equipment and departmental procedures. Yes, the room in which Steve Owens was interrogated did contain functional equipment for videotaping—three VCRs, one generally used for recording, one for playing, and one for copying tapes. Crime victims were sometimes videotaped, particularly victims of child sexual assault. But department policy was *not* to videotape interviews of criminal defendants.

~ ~

Judge Diltz announced, "Well, members of the jury, that concludes the evidentiary phase of this trial." A collective sigh of relief was nearly audible from the jury, if not from the judge himself. He continued:

> I will remind you one more time . . . you are not to discuss the case amongst yourselves, not to begin your deliberations at all. We still have to do the final arguments and Court's instructions on the law before the case is ready to be deliberated on.

At 3:12 p.m. Diltz dismissed jurors early. The real work for the jury would begin the following day.

Photos

View of apartment from front door, taken about a week after the stabbing. Two days after the fatal brawl, Greg Hoefman moved back in, cleaned up, and replaced broken furniture, perhaps hoping to restore his life.

Left: Demolished coffee table and lamp; picture knocked off wall.
Right: Flattened lampshade (foreground).

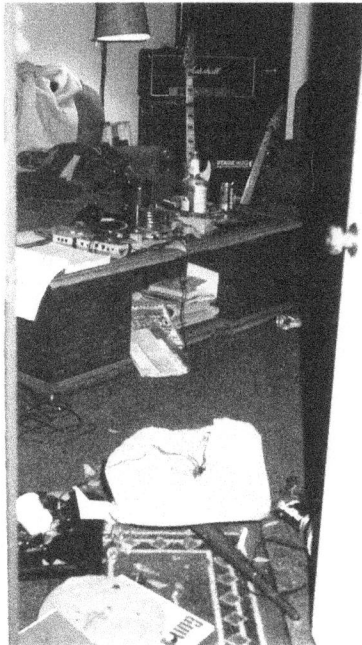

Table reveals Tom and Steve's activities. Ate Fudge Sticks, smoked cigarettes, listened to music, played videogames and, of course, drank the bottle of brandy. Needle-nose pliers that Steve used to try to repair Tom's guitar can be seen at upper-left, near video joystick. Ashtray (in front of bottle) is smashed.

Steve Owens's chemistry set in his bedroom. Note the two microscopes and the thirty bottles of chemicals. In searching the apartment, local police incorrectly considered this a probable "methamphetamine lab."

Window in Steve's bedroom. One of two telescopes of Steve's. Sword was leaning against the curtain, just to the right of the telescope.

Steve was not known for his housekeeping. This mess, however, was the result of the police's zealous search of his room.

This homemade cape, hanging in his bedroom, reflects Steve's interest in the cosmos. He occasionally wore it in public. It was one of his two prized possessions, the second being his collector's sword.

Steve built this "gangbuster"—a modified shotgun shell—to use if he were chased on city streets. When thrown into the air, the streamer keeps the device vertical. If the shell lands on a concrete surface, it explodes upward. He never had to use it, but tested it and concluded it was an effective deterrent, but not a weapon.

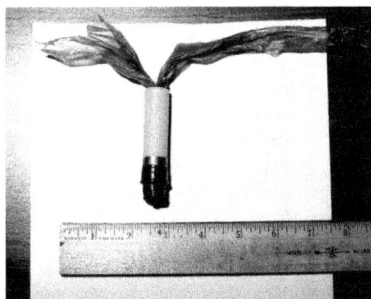

Snow "message" found at neighboring apartment complex during police investigation. "U DIE! I'M AREADY [sic] DEAD. ThAX X!" Prosecution claimed the message represented a confession. Others claim it is merely an example of cryptic statements for which Steve Owens was well known. Owens has no memory of writing the message but doesn't deny he did.

Left: Owens's bedroom door, as viewed from narrow hallway.
Right: Backdoor area of kitchen. Door on left leads to basement, door on right to outside. Owens claimed presence of recycling, garbage, and telescope (see tripod legs) eliminated door as a practical exit.

Top: Overview of area, from southwest. Owens's apartment was in the building in the foreground.

Bottom: Side view of four-unit apartment building.

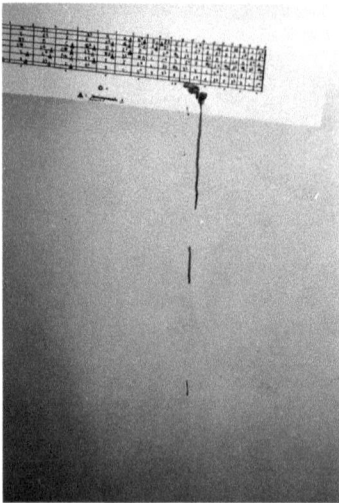

Top: Front door of apartment, belies havoc inside.

Right: View of living room wall, from front door.

Bottom: Fretboard chart on wall reveals guitar interests of Owens. Just before being stabbed, Tom Azinger grabbed the sword and sustained deep wounds to his hands. Blood stain on fret chart shows Azinger leaned against the wall before turning and leaving through the front door.

Fatal sword at crime scene, on living room floor near front door. Blood on the blade covers about 7 inches from the sword's tip.

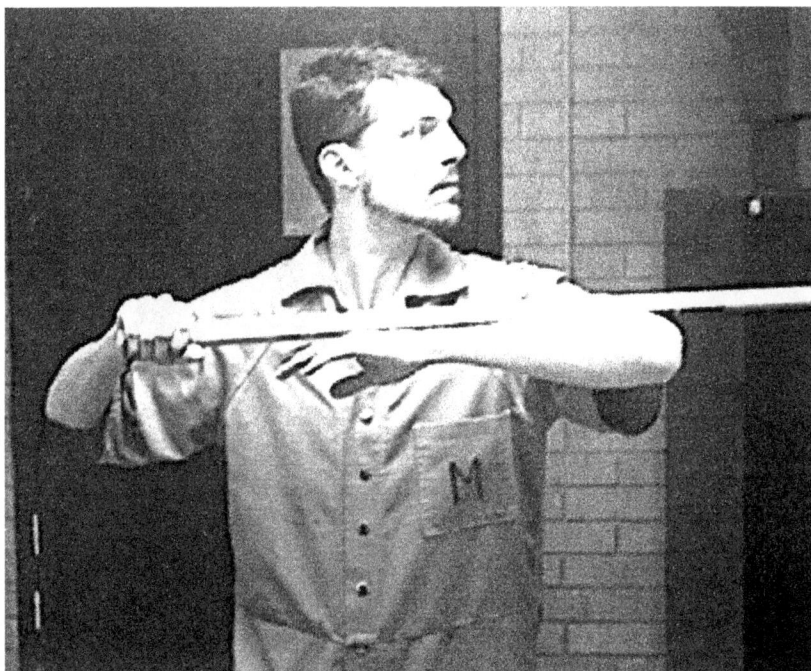

At police station after arrest, Owens demonstrates the defensive pose he assumed seconds before "poking" Azinger. He would also re-enact this stance in the courtroom before the jury.

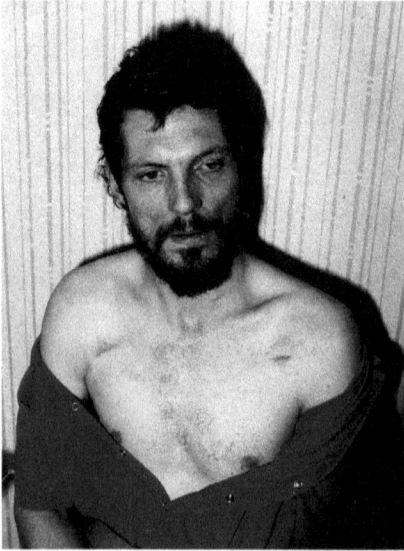
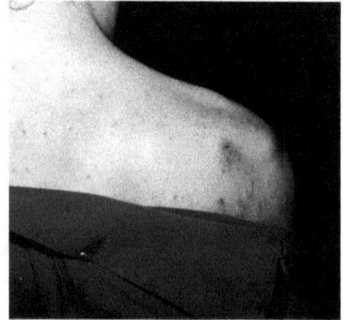
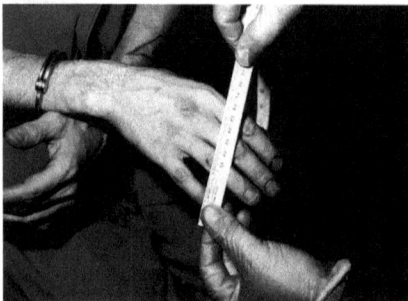

Injuries sustained by Owens during fight with Azinger. In addition to abrasions to his forehead, chest, shoulder, and hand, he sustained bruising to his lower back.

Steve Owens, about age 18.

Freshman teammates: Steve Owens #22 and best friend
Patrick Jeanquart #60. Although Steve hated sports, he
tried football in an attempt to "fit in."

Artwork by Steve Owens

Steve Owens typically uses ballpoint pens for his artwork. The Christmas card represents his idealized family. He scavenges feathers from the prison recreational yard, then paints them. Note owl (feather at right) and cardinals (faint, feather on left).

14

Verdict

Tim Funnell had a decision to make. He recalled his opening statement to the jury, a week earlier. *After all the evidence is in . . . I'll ask you to find the defendant, Steve Owens, guilty of first-degree intentional homicide.* In his own mind he had proven his case. But what about the jurors, what if they were not convinced beyond a reasonable doubt? It was his first murder trial. A conviction would be a feather in his cap, but an acquittal would be devastating.

The decision for the jury did not have to be one or the other, however. Funnell could ask Judge Peter Diltz to read instructions for lesser charges. In the event the jury could not decide unanimously for first-degree homicide, it could still convict Owens of a lesser charge and send him to prison for a long sentence.

After the jury had been dismissed on Day 6 of the trial, Funnell and Nila Robinson met with Judge Diltz to discuss the jury instructions. Diltz asked Funnell what charges he was asking for. He answered, "At a minimum . . . first-degree intentional, second-degree intentional, and second-degree reckless."

Robinson had anticipated Funnell's strategy of asking for practically everything, and she countered:

> Just because Wisconsin [law] allows other forms of
> homicide [in addition to first-degree intentional]
> doesn't mean it is always appropriate to offer a
> smorgasbord of [lesser] offenses. . . . When you
> give the jury so many possibilities, they are more
> likely to convict on something. . . . For these rea-
> sons we are asking you to submit only the instruc-

tion for first-degree intentional charge, along with self-defense.

The two attorneys dueled for over an hour, before Judge Diltz finally gave his decision. He sided with Funnell.

~ ~

"Thank you for the time and attention you have given to this case and for your patience during these seven days of witnesses and testimony." So began Tim Funnell in his closing arguments on Day 7 of the trial. He proceeded to spell out the case for first-degree intentional homicide:

> There are three critical elements: cause, intent, and self-defense. . . . There is no reasonable doubt that the death of [Tom Azinger] was caused by the actions of the defendant. . . .

> Intent does not require any set length of time, not 5 minutes or 10 minutes or a bunch of planning. . . . It could be formed in the instant preceding the act. . . .

> The state does not have to prove motive, which is the reason someone does something. I only have to prove intent, their mental state at the time. . . .

> Moving on to self-defense, there are two types: perfect and imperfect self-defense. If you find perfect self-defense, then the defendant is not guilty of any homicide. . . . When you look at perfect self-defense, it's the "reasonable person test." What does that mean? The reasonableness of the defendant's beliefs [must be judged by] what a person of ordinary intelligence and prudence would have believed . . . under the circumstances existing at the time of the alleged offense. Ask yourselves not what he actually thought, but what a reasonable, prudent person would have believed.

Verdict

Funnell then turned to whether the defendant actually believed, one, that he was in imminent danger of death or great bodily harm and, two, that the force used was necessary to defend himself. He emphasized that the evidence showed Owens was not *afraid* of Azinger—rather he was *angry* at him. This was a key to the charge of first-degree intentional homicide. Without fear, there could be no claim of self-defense. He acknowledged, however, a reasonable jury might conclude Owens *did* act in self-defense. In that case, the jury must evaluate the *reasonableness* of his beliefs and actions.

By the end of his closing arguments, Funnell had covered a lot of ground, including a detailed discussion of reasonable doubt, circumstantial evidence and, of course, self-defense. His final request, though, was simple: "Ladies and Gentlemen, I ask you to go back to the jury room and find the defendant guilty. Thank you."

~ ~

It was Nila Robinson's turn. Like her legal opponent she began by thanking the jurors for their attention during the trial. Then she discussed speculation—what would have happened *if* X had occurred instead of Y. She employed a common metaphor—Monday morning quarterbacking—clumsily modifying it to reflect the present time of day and day of week.

> Question is not whether in some Tuesday afternoon quarterbacking we can consider any possible way this scenario could have turned out happier—without Steve being beaten up and Tom being dead.

Steve and Tom had scuffled on prior occasions, Robinson acknowledged, yet they remained friends. Tragically, things escalated. It was Tom, not Steve, who did the escalating, by refusing to leave the apartment, by closing the front door when asked to leave, and by "bringing the fight" to Steve.

> It's a tragedy that someone died. The jury instruc-
> tions do not require you to decide whether this
> was a tragedy, only: Was this a homicide? There is
> nothing you can do about the first tragedy, but
> convicting a person who does not deserve it would
> be a second tragedy, and you *can* do something
> about that. I ask you to return a verdict of Not
> Guilty."

~ ~

Judge Peter Diltz had served on the bench for many years, yet this was his first trial involving a charge of first-degree intentional homicide. A lot was at stake, certainly for the defendant. The judge had to get all of the instructions just right, but he also wanted to avoid long-windedness. The day before, Nila Robinson had expressed concern that very long instructions might lose the jurors—*glaze them over.* "The jury pays attention for about 45 minutes. Go much past 55, you're wasting your breath," she warned.

Slowly the judge began. He defined "homicide" for the jury and addressed the legal differences between its types and degrees. Then he went into considerable detail about self-defense:

> It is privilege to threaten or intentionally use force
> to prevent or terminate what he reasonably be-
> lieves to be unlawful interference with his person. .
> . . However, he may not use such force unless he
> reasonably believes it to be necessary to prevent
> imminent death or great bodily harm. . . . . or the
> unlawful interference with the person's property. .
> . . If the defendant reasonably believed he was
> preventing or terminating interference with his
> person or property . . . he is not guilty of any
> homicide.

Verdict

Diltz continued with legal distinctions between "perfect" and "imperfect" self-defense. Finally, the judge explained that although the defendant had no legal *duty to retreat* from a threatening situation in his home, the jury could consider whether such retreat was feasible.

Near the end of his instructions, Diltz reminded jurors of the gravity of their duty:

> You will not be swayed by sympathy, prejudice, or passion. You will be very careful and deliberate in weighing the evidence. And I charge you to keep your duties steadfastly in mind and render a just and true verdict.

It had not been a speed contest, he knew, but Judge Diltz might have been pleased to have completed his instructions in just over thirty minutes—less time than either attorney had used for closing arguments. Finally it was time to swear in the court bailiff, who escorted the jurors to their deliberation room. It was 1:45 p.m.

~ ~

By the time the jury marched into the courtroom with their verdict, Steve Owens had little if any hope of acquittal. His defender had made a reasonable effort on his behalf, he felt, but he doubted she had swayed the jury. Instead, it was the prosecutor who seemed to reign over the jury, and even the judge at times. Owens felt doomed.

By contrast, Robinson was optimistic she had convinced the jury of Steve's innocence. From the beginning she believed the case to be a textbook example of self-defense. Her burden had been simply to convince the jury her client had been in fear for his life—and reasonably so. He had acted to protect himself, and she expected the jury to see it her way.

~ ~

Fatal Sword

The jury took just four-and-a-half hours before informing Judge Diltz that it had reached a verdict. The fate of Steve Owens had been decided. At 6:47 p.m. on Tuesday, July 30, 2002, the twelve jurors filed into the courtroom and the verdict was read: Guilty of first-degree intentional homicide. It was exactly what prosecutor Tim Funnell hoped for, though perhaps more than even he expected.

15

Sentence

The verdict had been read, and the jury properly thanked and dismissed from duty. The courtroom had emptied, except for a few stragglers. But the drama was far from over.

In the jury deliberation room the court bailiff was performing her post-trial duties. Like a housekeeper she moved around the room, picking up discarded drinking cups, wadded up papers and candy wrappers, and the pencils and blank paper that had been made available to the jurors. As she was depositing the leftovers into the trash can, she made a startling discovery.

Inside the can was a stack of *printed* notes! Looking more closely the bailiff realized the papers included a definition of murder and a list of points related to the trial. Instinctively she knew what she had found was very likely a violation of the judge's reoccurring admonition to the jurors *not* to do any outside research on the case.

She suppressed her temptation to explore the notes further—this was a serious matter and her responsibility was to inform the judge immediately. In his chambers Judge Diltz was busy performing his own post-trial, judicial "housekeeping." The last thing he expected was a knock on his door by the bailiff. "Judge, we may have a problem."

The judge and bailiff then began going through the discovery, the contents of which would eventually be entered as exhibits into the trial record. Some of the items found in the jury room were unremarkable—a binder-clipped set of jury instructions and a pad with handwritten notes. Of considerable concern, though, were the other items, all typewritten: a timeline of the crime, along with a clipped set of copies; a definition of intentional first-degree homicide; and a page entitled "Was it self-defense?" Quickly the judge realized a juror had brought the extraneous material into the jury room, an action strictly prohibited. This could put the entire trial in jeopardy, and Diltz knew he would have to act swiftly and decisively to prevent a mistrial.

Diltz contacted the jury foreperson, who solved the mystery of which juror had brought in the notes. The judge then summoned both the juror and the jury foreperson back to court. Formerly jurors, the two were now witnesses and were duly sworn in. The judge began questioning them.

The juror admitted doing research at home, after the final day of testimony (Day 6) but before closing arguments and jury instructions (Day 7). He described himself as "well-meaning" and admitted he had gone too far in trying to be conscientious. He was simply preparing himself for jury deliberations and thought his online exploration would prove helpful to fellow jurors. After hearing the judge's instructions to the jury, however, he realized his notes would be unnecessary. He claimed not to have directly shared or distributed the information to other jurors.

The judge turned to the jury foreperson. Had any of the outside notes been distributed? "Not to my knowledge." Did the juror share his findings *verbally* with the rest of the jury? "Not directly, I don't think. He did participate actively in the discussions so he made his views heard."

Diltz was satisfied. Though the juror was out of line, his actions, and the typed notes, did not taint the jury deliberations. The verdict would stand. The judge recognized, of course, the defense would likely make it all a basis for legal appeal, but he was confident his ruling would be upheld.

~ ~

The sentencing hearing was held on August 13. The decision facing Judge Diltz seemed simple. According to Wisconsin law, he could sentence Owens to life in prison *without* the

Sentence

possibility of parole or *with* the possibility of parole. If he chose the latter, he had to pick a number between 20 and 25 years.

His decision was simplified by formal notice from the Department of Corrections—based on its pre-sentencing investigation, it recommended the possibility of parole in 25 years. Before deciding, though, Diltz would need to hear from the family members of Tom Azinger, both attorneys, and the defendant himself.

The judge noted his receipt of two letters in support of Owens (from Greg Hoefman's mother and aunt). Both extolled Steve's virtues, especially his kindness and tendency to avoid conflict with others. Then Tim Funnell took the floor.

The prosecutor spoke for several minutes, repeating several points from his closing arguments. He also reviewed Owens's criminal record and past incidents that revealed a tendency toward threatening violence. Finally Funnell addressed Owens's mental health diagnoses and treatment from various providers, but he argued that Owens seemed perfectly capable of controlling himself when it served his own purpose, such as when he was on the witness stand, defending his actions.

Then it was Lorine Azinger's turn to speak to the Court:

> I am the mother of the deceased. . . . When considering your judgment as to the sentencing in this matter, my family would like you to consider the following: [Tom] had his strengths and weaknesses as we all do. He would have given the shirt off his back if you needed it. He was always willing to help. . . . Tom loved to tease and bring a smile to those he loved. He was aware of his weaknesses and was attempting to get his life back on track.
>
> He was sensitive to the feelings of others. He didn't attend our Christmas celebration because he couldn't afford gifts for everyone. We are now faced with never having another celebration with Tom.

We hope your Honor will give Steve Owens the maximum sentence allowed by law. Please consider the pain, suffering, and anguish we have felt. In closing, I would like to thank all my family and friends for their support and prayers. And to Steve Owens's family, my thoughts and prayers go with you.

Judge Diltz asked Mrs. Azinger to introduce her family members present in court, so she named Tom's three siblings and his sister-in-law.

Next Nila Robinson took the floor to plead the case for Steve Owens. She began by acknowledging the pain of the Azinger family in the face of their tragic loss. But she quickly expressed:

> I don't think severe sentences make a family feel any better when they walk out of the courtroom. I acknowledge the family's anger, grief, and natural desire for revenge. Surely, to the Azingers the defendant must appear as an evil creature responsible for the loss of their loved one. . . . But there is a great deal more to Steve than just those very unfortunate moments in the apartment when someone lost his life.

Then Robinson began justifying her request that Judge Diltz make Owens eligible for parole after the minimum of 20 years, rather than 25 years.

> Corrections does not automatically let him out the door when he passes the year 20. They look at how he has behaved, who he has been in that institution. They can consider better than anyone who he has become at that time. . . . But there is no question Steve Owens will be a very different person. He's 41 years old now [later that month]. When he has been in prison for 20 years, he will be 61. Like all of us, he will have changed.

Sentence

Robinson continued by acknowledging Owens's psychiatric past, admitting his highly unusual belief system could, at times, border on delusional. Then she explained how his illness manifested itself on December 24, 2001.

> His illness has a primary characteristic of fear and distrust of others. Like most people who are afraid, it's expressed as anger, that's really what anger is for all of us, just fear. He has spent most of his life unsure that he could trust anyone. . . . Steve is a man who never hurt anyone before this, and he never wanted to hurt his friend that night. . . . He is very aggrieved about what he has done, is very sorry, finds it very painful to see the Azinger family in court, especially Mrs. Azinger, whom he likes, and knowing how they must feel about him. . . .
>
> Just let Corrections decide what to do with Steve in 20 years. He may have had a number of years of fairly stable mental health, or he may not. . . . If he performs badly in prison, they won't let him out in 20 years, or 25, or maybe 30.
>
> I ask the Court to set the minimum eligibility for [parole] at 20 years, and let Corrections make that decision in the future. Thank you.

It was time for Steve Owens to address the Court. Judge Diltz asked, "Mr. Owens, is there anything you would like to say prior to sentencing?" Owens spoke briefly:

> There's nothing I can say that would really matter, honestly. Whether anyone believes what I say, basically, doesn't matter either.

Owens then turned to the Azinger family. He paused, perhaps recalling ruefully how things had once been, when he had maintained a cordial friendship with Tom's mother while they were neighbors. He remembered once removing a fallen tree limb from her car, how she had gratefully thanked him.

Fatal Sword

Mrs. Azinger, and the whole family, I am very sorry
for your loss, about everything that happened.
Tom was my friend. I wish I could trade places
with him right now. If I could, I would for certain.
It's unfortunate. I didn't intend to do anything of
the like. I just want you to know that.

And to my mother, I'm sorry about everything.

~ ~

It was time for Judge Diltz to hand down the sentence, but
he had a lot to say before doing so. He summarized his
options, from eligibility for parole to a life sentence without
parole—"life is life"—which he rejected. "The State is not
asking for life and I don't think the facts of the case warrant
it." But instead of then sentencing Owens, the judge decided
to discuss in detail the process by which parole is requested
and how the request is handled.

Diltz was taking his time, but when he started giving his
own theory of the events on Christmas Eve, everyone alerted.

I do not believe that, when Mr. Owens went to the
bedroom and picked up that sword, he intended to
kill Tom Azinger. On the other hand, the jury's
verdict indicates that self-defense was disproved
by the State, and I concur with that.

Certain aspects of that night I find disturbing.
First, Mr. Owens's introduction of a lethal weapon
to the situation completely altered the whole
course of the disagreement between the parties. It
upped the ante and I don't really believe that was
necessary. Mr. Owens had other options.

He could have simply left. The risk was that the
victim could have torn up his apartment. . . .
Rather than get the sword, he could have gotten
out that door. He could have gone to the nearby
home of Lorine Azinger and said, "Your son is over
at my house, I'm afraid of him, he could be tearing

Sentence

the place up, I need you to call the police, or let me call them."

The judge drew a contrast between shooting a victim and stabbing him. Unlike pulling a trigger in a split second, inflicting the fatal stab wound to Tom Azinger required a "very purposeful, offensive thrust. And accuracy, right through the heart. It causes me concern."

Then Judge Diltz turned to the offender's character, specifically addressing his mental health history. He expressed sympathy toward Owens's "difficulties and everyday struggles," but then stated Owens should have done more to "look after his mental health," such as continuing to take prescribed medications, not drink or smoke marijuana, and not absorb himself to the point of obsession with science fiction and aliens.

At this point Steve Owens must have felt he was still on trial, with new "charges" being levied against him: his decision to stop taking medications he felt were harming him, his drinking and smoking pot, and even his interest in science fiction. Would it all ever end?

Judge Diltz seemed to be nearing his decision, yet he digressed again to address issues of public protection, crime deterrence, and once again, the mechanics of parole. Finally he delivered his sentence:

> In 20 years Mr. Owens will be 61. I think back to
> my own life and a lot has changed in 20 years. . . .
> I don't have any magic idea about a number, but
> I'm going to choose 24 years, Mr. Owens. You will
> then be 65 years of age. In our society 65 is a
> passing point, retirement, social security, Medi-
> care. It's a passing into a new phase of your life.

Owens knew he was passing into a new phase of his life, and it was *now*—the year 2002. He was ready to leave Door County behind, though he wasn't ready for prison. But first he had to listen to warnings from Judge Diltz: Do not refuse or neglect assigned duties in prison, avoid segregation status, do not file malicious lawsuits—do any of these things and the Court can extend the length of your sentence. Among the judge's final words to Owens were *Take your medicine!*

Diltz wasn't being facetious, he was being literal. In March 2002, several months prior to his trial and after being behind bars for more than sixty days, Steve had grown despondent. The legal maneuvering by his public defender didn't seem to be working, and a trial date was nowhere in sight. Out of desperation he twice intentionally injured himself, by ramming his head into a door and stabbing himself in the arm.

His behavior was serious enough to draw the concern of district attorney Tim Funnell. The prosecutor may have had personal concern for Steve, but he also worried Owens might be headed toward an NGI plea—not guilty by reason of insanity. Additionally, a conviction might be overturned on appeal for failing to address the defendant's mental status.

At Funnell's urging Diltz ordered a pre-trial psychiatric evaluation. Owens was found to be legally competent but after he was transferred back to county jail, he wasn't quite the same person. He was now on a heavy regimen of psychiatric medications that left him feeling drugged—fatigued, lethargic and, at times, apathetic. Trial observers had remarked that Owens did, in fact, often appear lethargic and disinterested, staring down at the defense table or out the window. Whether the jury took notice and considered his apparent apathy in their verdict cannot be known.

On the day he was sentenced, Steve Owens felt victimized in a variety of ways: by a psychiatric system that misdiagnosed and mistreated him and by a legal system that misunderstood him and his drastic actions on Christmas Eve of 2001. Now he was being condemned to the state penal system, potentially for the rest of his life.

16

Appeals and Letters

Steve Owens vigorously appealed his conviction. He might have appeared apathetic as a defendant in the courtroom, but as an inmate facing the harsh reality of life in prison, Steve energetically embraced his constitutional right to appeal. All of the sustained determination he could muster would be required for the complex, time-consuming process that would eventually span years.

Three weeks after his sentencing Owens filed a notice of intent to pursue "post-conviction relief," claiming he had not received a fair trial due to jury misconduct. At issue was the behavior of the juror who conducted research on his own and came to jury deliberations with notes and timelines to distribute to fellow jurors. Judge Peter Diltz properly held a hearing but declared that the activities of the juror were harmless. The judge's ruling could be legally incorrect, however, and that was the basis of Owens's appeal.

Legal appeals often proceed at a glacial pace, as Owens experienced. It took exactly one year from the date of sentencing before an evidentiary hearing was finally called to order by Judge Diltz, who denied the appeal nine days later. Owens immediately appealed to the Court of Appeals and eventually to the Wisconsin Supreme Court. In November 2004, his motion for a new trial came to finality—denied.

Owens then began an entirely different appeal, grounded on the claim he was being illegally detained due to trial error. The error in question was Judge Diltz's refusal to permit testimony regarding "specific acts of violence by the victim, acts known to the defendant." In pre-trial hearings Owens's defender had argued for the right to present such evidence, and she renewed her plea during the trial, all based on her interpretation of case law.

If Owens had prior knowledge of specific acts of violence by Tom Azinger, which he did, then his claim of being fearful for his life or safety would be more believable to the jury. The judge's ruling disallowed such a line of defense, because it would be too time-consuming and distract from the main issues of the trial. Now, Judge Diltz was being asked to reconsider his previous decision, to admit that he had been in error. To no one's surprise Diltz stuck to his guns and denied the motion for a new trial.

Owens appealed higher. He had spent more than five years and gone through three state-appointed attorneys to help with his appeals. At times he represented himself. Finally things were coming to a climax. On September 11, 2007, ironically the sixth anniversary of the 9/11 attacks, the Wisconsin Court of Appeals ruled against Owens once again. Still determined, he immediately petitioned the Wisconsin Supreme Court for a new trial. On December 20, the Court denied Owens, just as it had denied his previous appeal three years earlier. Steve Owens's battle with the legal system was finally over, and he was the loser.

~ ~

They may not have fully understood the complexities of the legal appeals, but following his sentencing the friends and supporters of Steve Owens were full of fervor. They were astonished and outraged by the verdict, although those who attended the trial could see the handwriting on the wall almost from the start. Some supporters felt Steve's actions on Christmas Eve were absolutely in self-defense and he should serve no prison time. Others felt he should pay *something* for his role in the death of Tom Azinger—say, eight years.

A letter-writing campaign began shortly after the trial. There were individual letters, plus a group letter signed by nine supporters, most of whom were well acquainted with both Steve and Tom. Steve's advocates faced two obstacles, though. First, they weren't sure *to whom* they should direct their impassioned pleas. Second, without legal training or experience in advocacy, they weren't sure *how* to express themselves. So they addressed their letters "To Whom It May Concern," and they spoke from their hearts.

Greg Hoefman wrote:

> I am writing for my friend Steve Owens who has been imprisoned for a most unusual situation. . . . Steve has no past history of violence making this an act that is totally uncharacteristic. He pleaded for the trial to be moved to a different venue, knowing that he was guilty until proven innocent in this small town [Sturgeon Bay]. And he was right.

> Tom, the victim, was a lifelong friend of mine as well, I was best man at his wedding, so you see this is not one-sided.

> At first I believed Steve would receive some jail time, but I never would have believed a first-degree charge would be [levied] against him. Considering all the evidence, how could the jury have handed down a first-degree? Perhaps involuntary man-slaughter, but nothing more.

> The lawyer appointed for Steve was [ineffective]. The [district attorney] on the other hand was charming, witty, and charismatic. He presented the case in a way that made the jurors take inter-est in what he was saying. I truly believe the DA was stunned by the first-degree verdict. He pushed for it, just hoping to get a lesser charge.

> Steve never lied or changed his story in any way. His testimony undoubtedly showed that this was NOT intentional, [at least not to a] reasonable doubt.

I issue a challenge to anyone—attorney, law student, judge, or even [the governor of Wisconsin] to review this case or the trial transcripts. I know there is at least one soul out there who can make a difference.

With hope, Greg Hoefman

Becki Hoefman, Greg's sister, wrote:

I am writing regarding my friend Steve Owens, who was wrongly convicted of first-degree intentional homicide.

I have been friends with both Steve and Tom Azinger for over twenty years. Steve has always been passive, respectful, and non-confrontational. Tom was the opposite: aggressive, arrogant, and violent.

I cannot believe the judge did not allow the jury to hear about Tom's violent past. *This was the most important information!* [emphasis added] The justice system should give the jury *all* of the facts. The judge and the [prosecutor] should not pick and choose what the jury can hear. . . .

How can Steve be charged with first-degree [homicide] if there was only one [stab] wound? If he intended to end a life, there would definitely be more than one wound.

Please review Steve Owens's case and correct this injustice, please.

Sincerely, Becki Hoefman

Bob Raynier wrote:

This is an attempt to get justice for Steve Owens, a good friend and caregiver to me.

I spent 18 months in Vietnam and was sent home due to injuries. I am now paralyzed from the neck down due to so much shrapnel, and I have an eventually fatal disease. Steve Owens helped care for me when others quit and left me helpless. He was very caring and compassionate and a few times actually saved my life by getting me to the hospital as I was struggling for air.

There is no way possible Steve Owens would have intentionally harmed anyone. He was always compassionate and cared about life. This whole trial was a miscarriage of justice from the start. "Intentional" is a very strong word and was applied inappropriately in this case.

The very thought that we cannot protect ourselves in our own home is unthinkable, especially knowing [Azinger's] history of violent behavior, which was suppressed from the jury.

Please reconsider the facts and events of this episode and restore justice for Steve. . . . Thank you.

Robert Raynier (handwritten by a friend)

Another supporter wrote a lengthy letter "To Someone Who Cares about Justice." Several points were expressed, many similar to those stated in the above letters. This advocate contended that Steve Owens knew he couldn't get a fair trial in Door County, but when he asked his lawyer for a change of venue, she assured him it was not necessary. The writer also complained about the court's handling of the improper notes discovered in a wastebasket in the jury room.

The target of the letter was the governor of Wisconsin, and the hope was: "Please reconsider the sentence and issue a pardon or shorter sentence in the name of justice and fairness." The supporter waited and waited, but received no response.

~ ~

Fatal Sword

Long after the initial letters of supporters had been written and while the legal appeals were slowly winding their way through the courts, two particularly dedicated individuals continued to do everything they could to obtain the justice they felt Steve Owens deserved. Juanita*, Greg Hoefman's aunt, regularly wrote Steve during his first years in prison and visited him as often as she could. The two became close friends. She had heard of the Innocence Project and was hopeful others could see what Owens's supporters saw—that Steve was an innocent person wrongly convicted and incarcerated.

Made famous by Barry Scheck, one of the attorneys who represented O.J. Simpson, the Innocence Project seeks to exonerate wrongly convicted inmates. Juanita's application to the Project was submitted in 2004, but she received no response until 2007. The organization apologized for the long delay, citing its receipt of thousands of letters every year. The Owens case did not fit their criteria for consideration, because Owens was at the scene of the alleged crime and DNA evidence was not relevant.

Becki Hoefman also tried repeatedly to intervene for Steve. First, she wrote the Center on Wrongful Convictions (CWC), which claims to be at the forefront of the movement to reform the criminal justice system and to rectify wrongful convictions. Each year the CWC receives thousands of letters on behalf of inmates across the nation. Apparently they are unable to answer every one, as Becki never received a response.

Next, Becki wrote Legal Action of Wisconsin. The managing attorney wrote back, informing her that the program does not represent incarcerated persons. At least the response was timely, and they kindly referred her to Legal Assistance for Institutionalized Persons (LAIP), based in Madison, Wisconsin. So Becki immediately wrote LAIP. One of the goals of that program is to provide law students with a volunteer experience in "law in action." Unfortunately for

Appeals & Letters

Becki it was another case of *law inaction.* She received no response.

Steve Owens himself wrote to every entity in Washington, D.C., he could think of. Without access to a computer or even a typewriter, he went to great pains to compose a letter reflecting the legal issues—"injustices," in his words—involved in his case. He used his very best handwriting and attempted to ferret out errors of spelling and punctuation. Additionally he tried his hardest not to ramble, a difficult challenge for him.

The product was a two-page letter outlining his grievances about his trial. The highlights of his plea follow [edited for brevity].

> I am not some important person, I'm not rich or famous, I've had a few minor infractions with the law. . . . But I'm not a murderer. I acted out of self-defense, pure and simple, nothing more and nothing less. . . .
>
> Our justice system is supposed to be about the "truth and nothing but the truth." When I was interrogated, I chose to tell the absolute truth, because I trusted in the system, as I had been raised to by my parents.
>
> But the prosecution twisted everything and used my own words against me. Instead of the truth coming out in court, the jury ignored my self-defensive actions and convicted me. I now face a life sentence in state prison.

Owens sent his letter to every important person and agency he could think of, including: the US Pardon Attorney, the Federal Bar Association, the Federal Judicial Center, his US Senator, the Judiciary Committee of the US House of Representatives, the US Office of Government Ethics, and the FBI. He received no responses.

17

Tom and Steve

A cauldron was brewing on East Spruce Court. Tom Azinger and Steve Owens were flawed individuals—like all of us! But their flaws were serious ones, and on Christmas Eve 2001, they combined in a toxic way. Who was the master chef—Chance or Fate? Regardless, the recipe was a disaster.

Tom could be witty, funny, and charming. People who knew him best were quick to identify his most lovable qualities. His fun-loving nature was infectious—he loved to laugh and draw others into his good times. Moreover he was always willing to help, to offer a hand to a friend or stranger. That he had plenty of male friends, and little trouble attracting girlfriends, was no accident. As a skilled electrician he had the potential for solid employment. In many ways he had a lot going for him, but there were downfalls as well.

A close relative lovingly recalled two particular traits: "Tom loved to smoke marijuana, and he had a knack for choosing the wrong women." Others would say his biggest problem was alcohol, not marijuana. And relatives of the women who loved Tom would question *their* choice of him.

If Tom had a flaw greater than excessive drinking, it was his belief that he was *always* right. Everyone who knew Tom agreed—he *never* lost an argument, because he never conceded anything to anyone. He would argue, argue, argue until his opponent gave up. On occasions when he found himself kicked out of a bar, it was due to his argumentativeness more than unruliness.

One incident in particular illustrates Tom's duality—his playful nature countervailed by a persistent, menacing side.

Tom and Steve

Tom was drinking at a bar with his close friend Dean. After several drinks Dean decided enough was enough, and he told Tom he was ready to go home. Tom decided otherwise. He grabbed Dean's car keys and refused to return them. Dean tried to joke along, asking nicely for his keys, but Tom refused. Dean got angry and aggressive. Tom playfully eluded him. The bartender called the police. By the time they arrived Dean had wrestled his keys from Tom and was ready to drive away. But the police arrested Dean, even as Tom poured on his charm and escaped scot-free. Dean was found guilty of disorderly conduct, ironically by Judge Peter Diltz.

Tom's history of drinking and partying dated back at least to age fourteen. Whether he was motivated primarily by excitement or by demons is unclear. In eighth grade his best pal was killed tragically in a gruesome farm accident, and this affected Tom deeply. His home situation was at times chaotic, due to his father's heavy drinking and parental discord that eventually ended in divorce.

If young Tom were looking for an anchor, he found it in the son of a fisherman. Greg Hoefman became his best friend in high school and would remain so forever. Unfortunately Greg himself was a heavy drinker. Additionally, he seemed incapable of offering Tom much dating advice, especially when Tom began dating, and later married, Gary's cousin Trenda.

Sadly their long friendship ended with Tom's tragic death in Greg's apartment. That Greg would continue to live in the apartment for eight more years after the tragedy seems unfathomable. Perhaps it was his way of paying homage to his two best friends—one dead and the other in prison, possibly for life.

~ ~

Steve Owens has serious flaws of his own, and they undoubtedly contributed to the tragic events on Christmas Eve. A highly distrustful person, Steve is continually suspicious of the motives of others. He can readily perceive a dismissive slight as a real slam against him.

I recently asked Steve to rate his degree of trust on a 0-100 scale, with 0 = highly distrusting, 100 = highly trusting. Without hesitation Steve exclaimed, "A zero!" Two concrete examples illustrate his extreme wariness. Steve told me that in his days of driving, he always *backed* his car into parking spaces, a common practice by some but a puzzlement to others. Why, Steve? His measured response was, "You never know when you might have to get out of there in a hurry!"

Steve invented what he called a "gangbuster." It involved rebuilding a shotgun shell and attaching a kite-like tail designed to keep the shell vertical when thrown into the air. If all worked as planned the shell would land on a concrete surface—a road or parking lot—and explode. The buckshot would be expelled skyward and be unlikely to harm anyone, though it would provide a mighty scare. What was the purpose of the gangbuster? Only someone who expected to be bullied or harassed could give Steve's answer: "To scare away anyone who's chasing me."

Steve claims his extreme distrust and fear of others is the natural result of negative conditioning. A lifetime of losing—to bullies and systems—led to a heedfulness that is normal and adaptive, in his eyes. In the confines of a psychiatrist's office, where Steve found himself in 1986, these traits could readily be labeled paranoia.

Besides distrustfulness, another core characteristic of Steve's is honesty. Advise children to always tell the truth, and most might obey—until they realize the absolute truth can lead to unpleasant consequences. Steve learned from a very young age—mostly from his dad, he claims—to *always* tell the truth, except in the direst situations. He took the lesson to heart, rarely lying to anyone. Even today he can recite the circumstances of nearly every lie he ever told.

Steve's respect for truth and his distrust of authority clashed oddly when he was interrogated by police on Decem-

Tom and Steve

ber 25 and 26, 2001. He freely waived his Miranda rights and answered every question—"I had nothing to hide!" But in so doing he was naively placing his trust in his interrogator, whose purpose was to elicit statements that could be used against Steve in court.

Months later Steve ironically chose *not* to trust the person defending him. Nila Robinson, his defense attorney, advised him before trial to enter into a plea bargain—*save yourself from a possible life sentence.* Instead of trusting her, though, Steve chose to adhere to his most cherished principle—that the truth would set him free.

When Tom and Steve began their evening together on Christmas Eve 2001, their separate dreams seemed exhausted. Tom was thirty-six, and he had failed at four romantic relationships. He was out of work, cash-poor, and living with his mother. His only hope for a nice evening was to spend time with his best friend Greg, drinking away his problems with a bottle of fine brandy.

Steve, too, had given up on the future. He was forty and, like Tom, had seemingly been passed over by life. His two dreams in life were simple ones—to fly and to have a family. But his misdiagnosis of schizophrenia ruined his chances of becoming a pilot, or any other meaningful employment. What was the point in even trying?

Before Tom arrived Steve anticipated a quiet evening. He would play his guitar, maybe read or watch television, and wait for darkness. Then he would dress in dark clothing, don his night vision glasses, and head out into the surrounding woods and waterways, looking to see rather than be seen. Steve preferred spotting wildlife—*any* wildlife—rather than human life. There was nothing wrong with being alone, especially when surrounded by nature.

Neither Tom nor Steve got what they wanted, in life or on Christmas Eve. They got each other for five hours. Then Tom lost his life, and Steve lost his freedom.

18

Storytelling

Who told the better story? John Quincy Adams, the sixth President of the United States, famously stated: "In a courtroom, whoever tells the best story wins." It is a simple quote that applies aptly to the trial of Steve Owens. The jury was told the "story" of Tom Azinger's death in two versions. The facts of the story—its objective elements—were hardly in dispute. Instead, at the heart of it all was the concept of self-defense.

Self-defense is a basic—even pre-societal—right to protect one's self, and others. Children from a young age are taught to stand up to bullying, to fight back for themselves and others. They may be taught to defend against not only physical attacks but assaults of one's honor, or that of one's family. Self-defense is more than a legal right, more than a responsibility. It is honorable.

Every state in the US has codified self-defense as a legal defense to a charge of homicide. At trial the defendant has the initial burden of establishing that the statutory components of self-defense existed at the time of the alleged crime. Thereafter the prosecution bears the burden of proving otherwise. In the case of Steve Owens, he and his attorney had to convince the jury that he acted in self-defense. Prosecutor Tim Funnell then had to prove he did not.

~ ~

Readers of this book have the opportunity to take seats in a hypothetical jury box. Were Steve Owens's actions that led to the death of Tom Azinger justified? Did Owens act out of fear

Storytelling

of "death or great bodily harm"? If so, were his fear and his resulting actions reasonable?

What do I, the author, think? I have lived with the Owens case for nearly two years, interviewing people, researching details of events, listening to sworn statements of character witnesses, and even reading all 1913 pages of the trial transcript. Finally, I have exchanged dozens of letters with Steve Owens, talked to him by phone frequently, and interviewed him in prison a dozen times.

Some of my conclusions are unwavering. First, I believe Steve Owens when he claims, as he always has, that he feared for his life: "Tom was in a murderous rage. One of us was going to die that night." Second, I agree with Judge Diltz when he stated during sentencing that he did not believe Steve intended to kill Tom. But perhaps most critically, I find it difficult to accept that Steve acted prudently when he introduced the sword to the situation rather than fleeing the scene. It is true, by law, that a person acting in self-defense has no *duty to retreat* from a life-threatening encounter. On the other hand, he is required to act reasonably. Again I am influenced by the judge's assessment: Steve had nonlethal alternatives available to him, such as scrambling from the apartment in any way possible.

It is the issue of reasonableness that makes me toss and turn at night. Steve had a history of being bullied, dating back to his childhood. He learned to cope by suppressing fear and instead expressing anger. Sporadically he fought back when necessary. It is easy to see how this longstanding response to threat may have come to the forefront in his battle with Tom.

On the other hand, anyone who knew Tom recognized that his extreme argumentativeness could occasionally result in violence. He seemed to enjoy getting under people's skin. His friends and family had little choice but to accept, or tolerate, this side of Tom. One close acquaintance colorfully described him this way: "He could be a real pony's patoot."

Fatal Sword

Steve knew Tom as well as almost anyone did. He was familiar with his personality and fully aware of Tom's prior "specific acts of violence," which were inadmissible in court. What *was* allowed were photos showing Steve's injuries— mostly abrasions and contusions, plus a small cut on his hand. In contrast, extremely graphic photos of Tom's autopsy revealed a deep wound to his chest and lacerations to his hands. The pictures alone hardly tell the whole story of the deadly encounter, yet they undoubtedly helped sway the jury toward a guilty verdict.

Whether Tom was really posed really to kill Steve on Christmas Eve, or merely being a patoot, is impossible to determine. But I believe Steve truly feared for his life. Tragically, when he made the fatal decision to draw his sword, his judgment was impaired by panic, and alcohol.

~ ~

Who, then, told the story better? One could focus on either the two differing *versions* of the story, or on the *who*—the two storytellers. A common legal wisdom applies: If you can afford it, hire the best local attorney available. Steve Owens could afford no attorney, so he took the attorney assigned, and she was hardly local. It is unlikely that any of the jurors had ever heard of public defender Nila Robinson, from the distant village of Shiocton, Wisconsin. Prior to the Owens case she had represented criminal clients in Door County only three times (including twice before Judge Peter Diltz). None of these cases was high profile and none went to trial.

On the other hand, it is hard to overestimate the degree to which jurors were familiar with prosecutor Tim Funnell. Tim grew up in Sturgeon Bay and graduated from the local high school in 1987, seven years behind Steve Owens. Steve's high school years were marked not by accomplishment but by being bullying and serving occasional suspensions. By contrast, Tim was an absolute star—a gifted athlete and accomplished student. His high school career was filled

Storytelling

with sports—baseball, basketball, and football—and a wide variety of clubs, including: Letterman, Future Teachers, National Honor Society, and Academic Team. He received the Navy ROTC Scholarship Award. And he was popular, as evidenced in part by his election to the student council and his selection to the court of the Sadie Hawkins Dance.

That's not all! Tim Funnell was elected All-School President. On the first page of his senior yearbook, Tim is shown posing with "President Ronald Reagan." To the unwary, Reagan appears to be mixing it up with students at the local high school! The inside joke is that the image of Reagan is actually a life-sized, cardboard cutout. Still, some of Tim's classmates might have envisioned their class star as a future President.

Rather than politics Funnell pursued law as his chosen profession. Classmates and local citizens who admired Tim's impressive high school career likely followed his pathway through college and law school. In 1998, he campaigned as the "local candidate" for Door County District Attorney. Though he ran against the incumbent, he was elected in a landslide. When DA Funnell stood before the jury in the trial of Steve Owens, then, it is fair to assume most of the jurors knew him and probably admired him. As the "storyteller" for the state, he undoubtedly had an immeasurable advantage over the storyteller for the defense.

Prosecutor Funnell had five days during the trial to persuade the jury that Owens acted out of anger, that he intentionally stabbed Azinger to death, that self-defense had nothing to do with it. Defense attorney Nila Robinson then had to prove otherwise. Although she presented almost a dozen witnesses, they were handcuffed from saying anything about Azinger's "specific acts of violence." How could the jurors understand what Owens knew from years of interaction with Azinger?

As his own witness, Owens testified for several hours, with the ultimate goal of persuading the jury that he stabbed his friend not out of anger, but out of fear. His intention was not to kill Tom but to drive him from the residence. Prosecutor Tim Funnell would have the last word during closing arguments, though. Like a surgeon, he systematically dissected Owens's testimony and the summary arguments of the defense. In the end he asked the jury to believe his version and convict Steve Owens of first-degree intentional homicide. And they did.

~ ~

Immediately after being stabbed by Steve, Tom took a big step backwards and yelled, "You fucker!" Though very angry, Tom likely realized things had gotten out of hand, that a fight had finally gone too far. He then pivoted to his right and placed his left hand on the wall for support, before taking three or four steps to the front door. He turned the inner knob with his bleeding right hand, opened the door, and crossed the threshold, taking the six-inch step down to the concrete porch slab. He looked across the yard at his destination—his mother's house 140 feet away—likely understanding he had to get there in a hurry if he had a chance of surviving. But his interaction with Steve was not quite over.

Instead of stumbling immediately across the lawn, Tom performed a simple but meaningful act. He turned back, grasped the doorknob, and pulled the door closed. What was he thinking? Was it mere habit, or a simple act of courtesy? Did Tom realize he might never again walk into his friends' apartment? Perhaps by closing the door he was symbolically trying to put things back in place, the way they had been minutes before. Even as he was losing blood from his chest and gasping for air, he might have been filling with remorse.

And what about Steve? By his own admission he had been very angry at Tom, angrier than he had been for a long time. He claimed he thought he had only nicked Tom's clothing, or perhaps poked him only an inch. But his actions in the next few seconds suggest he too may have felt sudden remorse. He walked to the door Tom had just closed. Opening it, he called out to Tom, offering him words of conciliation: "I'm leaving for a while and I'm going to leave the door open. Come back anytime and get your shit," meaning Tom's guitar, duffle bag, and new jacket. In other words, *You're still welcome, my friend.*

~ ~

Today Steve Owens continues serving his life sentence in the Wisconsin prison system. He has a minimal work assignment, but he is primarily occupied with trying to cope with long boring days of prison routine. He spends hours at a time engaged in his artwork, playing his guitar, or reading, until even those activities eventually exhaust his interest. During his prior life of freedom, he loved nothing more than to investigate his natural world, in solitude. He would explore the heavens with his powerful telescope, soar into the skies in his homemade glider, plunge deep waters with a fishing line, and roam the outdoors in the middle of the night. There was no greater joy than the combination of nature, science, and tranquility. It is all gone now.

Owens is housed in a medium security unit at a very large state prison. There are one hundred inmates on his unit, and twenty-three other such units throughout the prison. He is generally free to come and go from his cell, watch television when he wants, socialize on the unit, or go to the arts room or library. There is a recreational yard but he generally avoids it, unless he goes hunting for bird feathers to incorporate into his artwork. Arguments and fights happen spontaneously in the yard, and Steve prefers to be alone or to interact with the few inmates he knows and trusts.

At night he looks out of his cell window onto the Wisconsin sky, hoping to see an occasional bird fly by. The dark endless sky offers hardly any hope. Recollections of happier times in his past are clouded by tortuous memories. He can't stop his mind from snapping back to 2001, to the fateful Christmas Eve. There is no peace, only the continual realization that life is fragile, that it can change forever in a matter of a few desperate seconds.

Steve will be eligible for parole in 2024, but there is no guarantee that he will ever set foot outside of prison. I ask him, "What would you do differently if you could re-live the night of December 24, 2001?" Though he has asked himself the same question a thousand times, he still pauses sorrowfully. Then he tries to put into words how everything went so terribly wrong, steadfastly contending he was in fear for his life. "The way things were going, one of us was going to die. I wish it had been me instead of Tom."

Source Documents

The following source documents offer details about events described in *Fatal Sword*. The documents have been excerpted and edited slightly, for the purposes of brevity, clarity, and readability.

Source Document 1
Police Reports. December 24-25, 2001

A. Reporting Officer (R/O): Deputy James Valley, Sturgeon Bay Police Department (SBPD). Report typed 12-26-2001.

On Dec. 24, 2001, at 9:20 p.m. R/O heard [police] dispatched to East Spring Court due to a stabbing. Dispatch stated that the subject's mother called, and he was stabbed in the chest . . . bleeding profusely and going unconscious.

R/O arrived at 9:25 p.m. and met with Sgt. Gary Rabach (SBPD) at apartment where stabbing occurred. Observed large amount of blood spots on porch and [front] door. Rabach called inside house numerous times that police were here and for anybody to come out. Based on situation and blood present, R/O and Rabach entered residence for safety of anybody else who was possibly injured. Upon entering front door into living room, it appeared a fight had taken place in living room . . . appeared to be broken ashtray on floor and numerous items scattered throughout, and possibly a broken table on the floor. Then joined by Officer Waterstreet and Deputy Fuerst. . . . Cleared kitchen area, west bedroom, and bathroom. Proceeded to clear east bedroom, observing desk with multiple chemicals and small bottle containers. Observed microscope with about 20-25 slides, appearing to be blood smears on each slide. Also a large Bunsen burner on floor and white powdery substance on desk. Left room and assisted clearing basement along with Waterstreet and Rabach. Observed large sword (3-4 feet in length) on living room floor on way out and saw blood on sword, approximately 3/4 of the way up. Also observed Mountain Dew can with burnt punch holes in it, suggestive of a makeshift marijuana pipe. Also observed blood on wall of living room. . . . Then heard yelling outside, telling the

144

Document 1

person to get on the ground. Rabach stated he would stay in apartment for security and for R/O to assist officers outside.

At cul-de-sac near apartment, Fuerst and Waterstreet had service weapons drawn on subject, lying prone on the ground. R/O drew his service weapon and covered Waterstreet while he arrested subject prone on ground. Fuerst searched person and placed his items in a bag. Waterstreet took suspect and transported him to police station. . . .

R/O spoke to District Attorney Tim Funnell, who had arrived on scene. R/O and Rabach briefed Funnell and explained possible lab in east bedroom, possibly a methamphetamine lab. Cannot confirm this, however, just by looking at the equipment. Was advised to contact Sgt. Terry Vogel, due to his drug expertise. Did contact Vogel at 10:31 p.m. and he arrived at the scene, where he was briefed. . . . Was later asked by Vogel to contact Pete Thelen of State DNE, which R/O did at 12:30 a.m. Explained situation and Pete said he would send four people to check out the lab . . . . At 2:16 a.m. DNE arrived, checked the residence, and concluded there was no meth lab. R/O cleared from the scene at 4:24 a.m.

B. Reporting Officer (R/O): Deputy Tim Fuerst (SBPD). Report typed 12-26-2001.

On Monday, 12-24-2001, at 9:21 p.m. R/O heard Dispatch call SBPD paramedics to an E. Spruce Court address for a stabbing. Arrived at 9:28 p.m. and met Sgt. Rabach and Deputy Valley. Officers Carl Waterstreet and Wendy Allen were also on scene. Rabach told Waterstreet and R/O to search the area for the suspect, identified as Steven Owens. R/O is familiar with Owens from past contacts.

As R/O and Waterstreet walked across the parking lot, [Greg Hoefman], Owens's roommate, drove up. Asked him where Owens may be and [Hoefman] stated he didn't know, he had just arrived home and was not there all day. R/O then observed a male walking towards him. It was Steve Owens crossing the parking lot toward R/O and Waterstreet. At 9:42 p.m. R/O, Waterstreet, and Valley drew their weapons, ordering Owens to lie on the ground with arms to his sides and head turned right. R/O tactically handcuffed Owens behind his back. As being handcuffed, Owens yelled several times at officers to shoot him and pull the trigger. Owens stated that officers should feel lucky to have him on our side and also made reference to recent terrorist attack and Osama bin Laden. After being searched and items taken off of body, Owens was escorted to Waterstreet's squad car, where he was placed in back seat at 9:42 p.m.

At 9:54 p.m. responded to Door County Memorial Hospital to assist and was told identity of the victim, [Tom Azinger] (white male, age 36). . . . Went into emergency room and observed numerous emergency personnel attending to victim. Apparent that victim was not breathing. ER personnel stated [Azinger] was not responsive since his arrival and had said nothing at the hospital. After all efforts to revive victim, he was pronounced deceased . . . .

C. Reporting Officer (R/O): Deputy Paul Keddell. Report typed 12-28-2001.

On 12-24-01, at 9:50 p.m. arrived at the Door County Jail to assist Officer Waterstreet with a prisoner. At 9:51 p.m. Waterstreet arrived at jail with Steven D. Owens, who was removed from backseat and given an outer pat down search. Owens began rambling about politics, terrorists, the FBI, and stated that police officers were "the good guys." R/O smelled intoxicants on Owens's breath. He had red, glassy eyes and slurred speech. He appeared intoxicated as he was unsteady on his feet and not making sense as he spoke. Owens had a strong body odor, as if he hadn't showered recently, and his appearance was unkempt.

Document 1

Owens was escorted into the secure portion of the jail and his shoes, socks, outerwear, and belt were removed. His pants and shirt were left on, and he was placed handcuffed in booking room holding cell. After cell door was closed, Owens slipped his wrists under his feet to bring his hand-cuffed wrists to the front of his body.

At approximately 10:30 p.m. the water was turned off to the holding cell. Shortly after, Owens became upset because water was turned off. R/O offered to provide Owens water from jail booking area. Owens refused, stating that R/O would put something in the water and he wanted the water turned on in his cell. Told Owens it would not be turned on and he could use the bathroom and we could provide him with water. Owens became loud over next ten minutes and rambled on about the Sheriff's Department being controlled by Jewish leadership and he wanted to speak to the FBI. Owens said he would hunt down family members and wished that our children would die of cancer.

At approximately 10:45 p.m. Lt. Baudhuin arrived and spoke with Owens, who appeared to recognize Baudhuin, became angry, and stated he did not want to see Baudhuin or Office Rockendorf because of previous incidents. Baud-huin told R/O to contact Community Programs to respond to the jail to speak with Owens. At 10:59 p.m. R/O had dis-patch page the on-call party from Community Programs. At 11:06 p.m. R/O was informed by dispatch that Callie Krauel from Community Programs would be responding in approxi-mately one-half hours. At 11:14 p.m. R/O was sitting at the booking desk and heard Owens state, "I suppose defending yourself in your own home is an offense now." Owens con-tinued on about not having water in his cell. Told Owens if he would cooperate R/O would provide him with water. Owens told R/O he would cooperate. Opened cell door and gave Owens two cups of water. Owens said he was sorry and was starting to sober up, said he was feeling better and he messed up when he first got in the jail. Owens said, "I don't mind you guys, just Baudhuin and Rockendorf." He appeared much calmer than before and was more rational and cooperative.

At 11:30 p.m. Callie Kraal from Door County Community Programs arrived and spoke with Owens through the holding cell door. R/O heard Owens state, "I stabbed him and I could have killed him, but I didn't." After Krause finished speaking with Owens, it was decided he would be placed on fifteen-minute [suicide] watch.

Sgt. Investigator Vogel arrived in the jail and asked Owens if he would like to speak with him about the incident. Owens agreed and R/O escorted him to interview room. After interview R/O escorted Steven back to [his cell].

Sgt. Dan Trelka and Officer Greg Zager arrived to transport Owens to Door County Memorial Hospital. R/O followed in squad car and Steven was escorted into the emergency room [ER] to receive medical treatment. Steven was initially examined by ER nurse. Two blood samples were taken and Officer Binish arrived to photograph Steven's injuries. He had two red marks, one on each pectoral muscle near the right and left shoulder. Steven said he did not have any other injuries. R/O asked Steven about the back of his head, which he stated earlier during the interview that he was struck by an object during the altercation. Steven said the back of his head didn't hurt, it was not a big deal. R/O and Officer Binish looked at the area and could not see any type of red marks, bumps, or bruising. ER physician arrived and examined Steven, who told him he did not have any injuries except for marks on his chest, said the area where the marks were did not hurt and he didn't even realize he had the marks until he was shown them at the jail. R/O told Steven to show the doctor the area on the back of the head where he was struck by the unknown object. Steven told doctor he did not have any pain in the back of his head, explained that when he turned away during the altercation, he was hit with a forearm in the back of the head, and not an object. Steven

Document 1

said that at the time it didn't hurt that much. Again said he did not have any discomfort in the back of his head as the doctor examined the area.

Upon completion of the medical clearance, Owens was transported back to jail by Sgt. Trelka and Officer Zager.

D. Investigating Officer: Thomas J. Baudhuin. Report dated 12-26-2001.

On 12-24-01 at about 9:45 p.m. I received a page notifying me of a stabbing incident that just occurred on E. Spruce Ct. After responding I was briefed by Sgt. Gary Rabach that [Tom Azinger] had been stabbed in the upper chest with a sword and suspect Steven Owens was responsible. I was advised that officers were initially called to the home of [Tom's mother] on E. Spruce Ct. where [Azinger] stated he was stabbed by Owens. Also, Owens had been located and taken into custody by officers on scene. At that point I spoke to [Tom's mother and brother], and she stated [Tom] had been stabbed by "Steve," who she believed to be Steve Owens. She stated that [Tom] was at Steve's house and when he returned home he was bleeding heavily from his chest area, that as soon as he entered her home he told her Steve stabbed him, to call the police, then he fell to the kitchen floor. At that point [Tom's brother] stated his desire to remove his mother to his home for the remainder of the night. Prior to leaving, [Tom's mother] gave SBPD control of her home to further this investigation.

At that point I viewed the kitchen and living area and noted a substantial amount of what appeared to be blood on the kitchen and living room floors. On the kitchen floor was a blood-saturated towel and a blue colored sweat shirt that had been cut from [Azinger] by EMS staff. Later I noted what appeared to be a cut mark on the sweat shirt just below the left sleeve, this cut relatively straight and about 1 in. in length. A similar cut was found on the shirt in the area that would have been along the back right of the shirt, possibly in the shoulder blade area.

I again spoke with Sgt. Rabach and was advised that officers had entered the Owens apartment fearing there may be others in need of assistance. Rabach stated that while looking into the apartment from the front porch, he could see substantial amounts of [apparent] blood on the door and floor area near the front door. Rabach stated that during a protective sweep he observed a chrome-colored sword on the living room floor, with apparent blood on its tip end. A substantial amount of bottled chemicals in the northeast bedroom, the chemicals and condition of that room consistent in appearance of a methamphetamine lab. Rabach had been in contact with DA Tim Funnell and advised to secure the scene, pending a request for a search warrant. At 11:45 p.m. I met Funnell in his office where a telephonic search warrant was drafted. The warrant was reviewed and signed by Judge Peter Diltz at 1:23 a.m. on 12-25-01.

I then met with Sgt. Terry Vogel, who was aware of the possible methamphetamine concern and had already contacted the Wisconsin Division of Narcotics (DNE). DNE was responding and had asked that, because of safety issues, no one enter until after their arrival and evaluation. At about 3:50 a.m. DNE arrived on scene. A set of keys from the suspect's personal property in the jail was used to unlock the rear door of the apartment, which allowed DNE to avoid the living room area. Following their entry I was advised by Senior Special Agent Ron Glaman that he did not believe that meth was being produced in the apartment but that many of the suspected chemicals found were consistent with meth production. After DNE cleared the apartment, Sgt. Rabach, Officer Binish, and I entered the residence with the instructions listed in the search warrant, a copy of which was left attached to the refrigerator in the kitchen. During the search, the entire apartment was sketched and measured, and listed items were later seized and placed into evidence.

Document 1

The sword found lying on the living room floor had a total length of approximately 38 in., including a blade of 29 in. and a handle of 9 in. What appeared to be dried blood was found from the blade tip through approximately the first 14 in. of blade. The blade's width at mid-shaft is approximately 1 in.

Only one phone was found, a cordless with the base station on the south kitchen wall. The phone was found lying on the half wall separating the kitchen and living room. The doors of the two bedrooms and the bathroom were all lock-equipped. The NW bedroom and the bathroom door had locks that would function properly. The bedroom leading to the NE bedroom [later determined to be Owens's] appeared to have a defective lock, which functioned properly when the knob was turned in one direction but would fail if turned the opposite way.

The living area was littered with rotting food, garbage, and empty liquor bottles. A table that apparently stood along the living room's north wall near the front door was completely destroyed, and the lamp that was apparently on this table was destroyed and found lying on the floor by the table. A coffee table near the center of the living room was found with one end almost touching the couch. The apparent blood trail left by [Azinger] after leaving the front door of the apartment was measured. That trail led directly to the front door of the residence of [Azinger's mother], the door-to-door distance being approximately 140 ft.

At about 7:30 a.m. canine unit from the Brown County Sheriff's Department arrived on scene. A trail of footwear impressions was found in the snow leading from the south end of the sidewalk in front of the Owens apartment, the trail traveling south up a large hill. These footwear impressions appeared to be made by a shoe very similar to the pair that suspect Owens was wearing at the time of his arrest.

I asked the canine handler to have his dog walk that trail for additional evidence. After a brief search I was summoned to an area near the Bayview Terrace apartment complex on S. Neenah St. located SE of Owens's apartment complex. I was then advised that some type of note had been scrawled in the snow on the lawn area of the Bayview complex. This note stated "U DIE! I'M AREADY [sic] DEAD. ThAX X!" This note appeared to have been recently scrawled, and in the area around the note were numerous footwear impressions consistent with the suspect's shoes. The canine handler stated that the trail leaving the Owens complex was followed to this note. Photographs of that note were taken by Officer Binish. The note appeared to cover an area approximately 20 ft. x 20 ft., the letters 12 – 18 in. in height.

Investigation continuing.

Source Document 2
Police Interrogations of Steven Owens
December 25 - 26, 2001

**A. Reporting Officer (R/O): Sgt. Investigator Terry Vogel.
Report typed 12-27-2001.**

On 12-24-2001 at 10:15 p.m. R/O was contacted by SBPD and asked to assist in a death investigation. Arrived at crime scene at 10:35 p.m. and met Sgt. Gary Rabach, Patrolman Guy Binish, and Deputy James Valley.

Was given an overview of crime scene and informed of possible meth lab. Valley stated that during a search, he discovered suspicious items, including bowls, glass vials and jars, white powder, a burner, and a microscope.

Contacted Wisconsin Department of Narcotics Enforcement (DNE) Special Agent Peter Thelen and requested assistance in identifying and possibly dismantling the lab. Thelen and three other officers would be arriving in about two hours.

While awaiting the DNE agents, met with Lt. Tom Baudhuin (SBPD) and District Attorney Tim Funnell. A decision was made for R/O to interview the suspect Steve Owens, presently incarcerated in Door County Jail.

At 12:20 a.m. escorted Owens from jail to the interview room located in lower level of Safety Building. R/O explained to Owens he wished to interview him regarding the incident at his residence. Prior to the interview, read him the Door County Sheriff's Department Notification of Rights form [including Miranda rights]. Placed it next to Owens where he could follow along as it was read to him. After each section R/O put a check mark next to it after Owens said he understood. Owens stated he understood his rights and signed the form indicating he was willing to talk to R/O at this time.

At start of interview, Owens showed great anger toward the victim and readily admitted getting into a fight with him and poking him with his sword. He repeatedly called the victim [derogatory names]. Owens felt he had every right to defend his home, at one point saying he wanted that fucker out of my face by any means necessary. Several times Owens asked why [Azinger] wasn't in jail, stating that fucker belongs in jail, not him. He also stated if I cut that fucker, he deserved it. After describing the incident, in which Owens said he stuck at [Azinger] with his sword, Owens told him, "Fuck you, [Azinger], you crybaby . . . ." and "Fuck you, you deserve it."

Requested Owens to explain what happened when he first woke up and then throughout the day until he was arrested. Owens said he does not know what time he woke up other than before noon. He just hung around his apartment with his roommate, [Greg Hoefman], until approximately 4:00 p.m. when [Hoefman] left to visit his mother.

Approximately 15–20 minutes later, [Tom Azinger] came to his apartment with a guitar and a backpack, which contained a half-full, large bottle of Aristocrat brandy. Owens stated he has known [Azinger] 10–15 years and has had him in his apartment numerous times in the past. Both began drinking directly out of the brandy bottle. While they were drinking, Owens said he changed the strings on [Azinger's] guitar and tried fixing the guitar's bridge. Throughout the evening they consumed the majority of the brandy until they started arguing about politics. Owens was not exactly sure what the argument was about, but when [Azinger] complained that he [Owens] made $6,000 per year [from monthly SSDI payments] because of the government, he had had enough. Owens ordered him out of his house.

He turned his back and got struck over his head by an unknown object. [Azinger] then shoved him, so he shoved [Azinger] back and they began wrestling on the ground. [Azinger] had him in a headlock, but Owens got out of it and began walking away. He looked back and saw [Azinger] reach down to grab an object. Owens went into his bedroom and

Document 2

obtained his sword, which was in a sheath next to his bed-room window. He took it out of its sheath and hollered at [Azinger] to get out of this house. He approached [Azinger] within four feet and told him to get out or he would stick him. [Azinger] laughed at him, which really angered him. Owens then stuck him with the sword but didn't feel he used a lot of pressure. As he was sticking him, [Azinger] grabbed his sword with his hand. Owens was unsure if [Azinger] cut his hand but thought he probably did. Owens pulled the sword back and [Azinger] began yelling at him as he backed away.

Owens thought [Azinger] was walking toward his [own] guitar and thought he was going to leave. Owens said he immediately threw the sword down and left the apartment. He said when he left, [Azinger] was still in his apartment. He [Owens] then walked directly down the hill toward the high-way. He felt he was gone about one-half hour. When he came back, he was confronted by police and arrested.

R/O requested Owens to put this statement into written form, which R/O did as given to him by Owens. After completing the statement, R/O read it back as Owens followed along. He agreed it was truthful and correct and signed each page to so indicate.

Throughout the interview, R/O detected the odor of intoxicants from his breath although observed no other signs of intoxication. Due to Owens's constant emotion of anger toward [Azinger], asked Owens to rate his anger toward [Azinger] on a 1–10 scale. Without hesitation, he said 10, stating he hadn't been that mad in years.

Also questioned him on any injuries he sustained during the incident. Other than a small cut on his finger, he did not feel he had any. Observed two abrasions to his chest area that appeared fresh. Owens responded that they were probably from the fight. He stated the finger cut was from his sword when the incident occurred.

During the interview, R/O had Owens draw a picture depicting his apartment and where the fight occurred. On the picture the two X's are where he confronted [Azinger] with the sword. Also of note is when he was identifying his bedroom, he wrote the word "Dead." Owens was then taken back to his cell where he agreed to turn over his clothing. He was then transported to the Door County Memorial Hospital where a blood test was taken.

On December 26 at 8:50 a.m. [approximately 36 hours after the stabbing], R/O and Captain Arleigh Porter reinterviewed Owens. Prior to questioning, R/O read him the Notification of Rights form, which he stated he understood and signed.

Prior to questioning, R/O told Owens that [Azinger] had died as a result of his injuries. After a lengthy pause, he stated, "I lost my mind, I asked him to leave."

Owens stated that prior to the argument he was sitting in a chair in the living room and [Azinger] was sitting on a couch. He remembered arguing about politics in general, but specifically recalled arguing about terrorists. Owens felt they [the US] should kill just the terrorists but [Azinger] felt they should kill everyone over there.

Again asked Owens to draw a picture of his apartment, including furniture. His description of physical fight was similar to his original statement. When asked where he poked [Azinger] with the sword, he felt it was about one foot below the left armpit. While poking [Azinger], he was looking more at his eyes, not his hands and did not see blood.

Owens was not sure when he sustained his finger cut but thought it was after the fight stopped.

When questioned about where he went after the incident, he changed his story from his original statement, now stating [Azinger] left the apartment first, holding his hands as if he had been cut. Owens said after [Azinger] left, he immediately put on a snowmobile suit and his hat and jacket and grabbed his night-vision binoculars. He exited his apart-

Document 2

ment, taking a left and then going up the hill to the business highway. He then headed south a short distance, then down the hill to Neenah Street, then south again to the highway. He crossed the highway but decided it was too late and he was too drunk to visit his mother, so he turned around and came back toward his residence. On the way back, he walked past the fire station, then walked behind the Bayview Terrace [apartments] and began wandering around in a wooded area. It was during this time he wrote in the snow with his finger, "U DIE! I'M AREADY [sic] DEAD. ThAX X!" He said he was blowing off steam when he wrote this.

On his way back to his apartment, he came out of the wooded area near the intersection of Spruce Court and Neenah Street. At this intersection he waved to [Greg Hoefman], who was coming [driving] home.

Owens then walked up Spruce Court, where he was confronted by the police. He told the police to shoot him because he figured he was going to spend the rest of his life in prison.

Questioned him about the shotgun shell found in his pocket, which was altered as an explosive. He stated he made the shell himself two or three years ago, for self-defense purposes. If people were after him, he would throw it and it would go off, scaring them.

Questioned about the large number of 22-calibre bullets found in his apartment, he stated he used to own a 22-calibre handgun, purchased approximately five years previously for $400. He used to shoot it with Brett Cloutier at the old Whitford farm where Cloutier lives. About one year ago he lost the gun in a swamp. About 2–3 months ago he was at Cloutier's residence shooting Cloutier's 22-cal. rifle and that is why he has all the bullets at his house.

Asked Owens the maximum the sword could have entered [Azinger's] body. He stated no more than one inch. Asked what should happen to him if [Azinger's] death was due to the stab wound. After a lengthy pause, he said five years in the mental institute, anything more wouldn't be fair.

Owens also talked about prescription medications he was taking. He stopped taking all medications in September, after using it for two months, because it made him feel "tweaky" and he couldn't sleep well. Before this, he had not taken medication for a seven-year period.

Assisted Capt. Porter in measuring Owens's height, which was 70 in. Porter took several photos of Owens to document his injuries, including abrasions to his chest and back and a bruise to his right shoulder, as well as a photo of his finger.

Attached to this report are the two drawings Owens made of his residence. On the drawing done Dec. 26, he shows his path from the fight to his bedroom to retrieve the sword and back to the confrontation.

Also attached is a second written statement taken from Owens at the time of the second interview. The statement was read back to Owens as he followed along. He signed each page, indicating it was accurate.

B. Investigating Officer: Lt. Thomas Baudhuin. Report dated 12-28-2001.

On 12-25-2001, I viewed the initial interview of suspect Steven Owens via closed circuit television. Interview was conducted by Door County Sheriff's Department Investigator Sgt. Terry Vogel. During interview suspect Owens referred to [Tom Azinger] as a [crybaby sucker] several times. When asked about the stabbing incident, Owens initially stated he only "poked" [Azinger] with the sword, it was not his intention to hurt anyone. As interview progressed Owens began to refer to the fact he "stuck" [Azinger] with the sword. When asked if [Azinger] said anything after being stabbed, Owens stated [Azinger] said "you cut me," and Owens replied "Fuck you then, you deserved it." Vogel asked Owens if he had been injured at all during incident, Owens then revealed a small cut on his knuckle and told Vogel "I cut myself on my own

Document 2

sword." When asked about the altercation that led up to the stabbing, Owens stated, "I wanted this fucker outta my face."

On 12-26-2001, I monitored a second interview of suspect Owens, conducted by Sgt. Vogel and Sturgeon Bay Police Capt. Arleigh Porter. Prior to that interview Owens was advised of his Miranda warning and waiver, at one point Owens told Vogel he did not have to read the Miranda form because he (Owens) was "pretty smart." Vogel continued with the Miranda warning, which was later waived by Owens. At start of interview, Owens was advised that [Tom Azinger] had died from the stab wound.

Owens stated that just before the stabbing incident he and [Azinger] were arguing about terrorism and each had different views on how terrorists should be handled. [Azinger] started the argument and he (Owens) just wanted [Azinger] out of his house. At one point [Azinger] said "I'm going to kill you," but he thought [Azinger] was "just kidding" when he made that remark. Once he had the sword in hand, he tried to "poke" [Azinger's] left side, stating he didn't want to hit him in a "vital spot." [Azinger] then turned and walked out the front door, appearing to hold his left hand as he left. Owens had no idea [Azinger] had been injured.

After [Azinger] left, Owens put on his snowsuit and decided to go for a walk, he was drunk and needed some air. When asked why he took his night vision scope, Owens stated he thought he would go for a walk and look for some deer with the scope. About 20 minutes later, he came walking up Spruce Ct. from Neenah St. toward his apartment. He noticed police, fire, and ambulance vehicles in the area, and thought to himself "What's all this?"

Vogel asked Owens about comments he made during his arrest, in which he insisted officers shoot him and that he (Owens) reportedly yelled that he should be shot because he was just going to jail for the rest of his life anyway. Vogel asked Owens why he thought he would be going to jail if it was his firm belief that no one had been injured in this

159

altercation, as he earlier stated. Owens had no response. It is also noted that Owens stated that when he left his apartment, he intentionally left the front door open in case [Azinger] wanted to "go back to get his shit." Also that as recently as a few months ago he was out target practicing with a firearm along with Brett Cloutier at Cloutier's farm outside Sturgeon Bay.

On 12-26-01 at 11:30 a.m. District Attorney Tim Funnell and I returned to the Owens apartment and used the suspect's keys to enter [with Owens's permission]. A black plastic scabbard, a box of Remington .22 caliber rounds, and a second gold-colored sword were seized and later placed into evidence. The Owens home was secured upon departure.

On 12-26-01 at 2:40 p.m. I attended the autopsy of [Tom Azinger] at St. Vincent's Hospital in Green Bay, Wisconsin, conducted by Dr. Witeck. Decedent's weight was 150 lbs., height 72 in. There was a superficial sharp force injury, 0.5 in. long on victim's right middle finger, also sharp force injury to left little and left ring finger. The injury to the left ring finger was significant, almost to the point of being severed. Point of entry of sword was along victim's left side, 55 in. from bottom of left foot, near left nipple line. Sword entered between 4th and 5th ribs, blade traveling 7 in. inward on a slightly downward angle. Blade traveled through both the heart and left lung, causing massive blood loss and injuries were ruled the cause of death.

On 12-27-01 at 8:05 a.m. I was in my office and received a phone call from a party identifying himself as [name, address, phone number redacted here]. Caller stated that on about December 17-18, 2001, he was at the Greystone Castle Tavern in Sturgeon Bay, where he was speaking with [Tom Azinger]. That he and [Azinger] talked about politics, that [Azinger] became upset when their political views did not agree, that [Azinger] got "heated" about the incident but that it went no further than that. Caller stated that [Azinger's] political views were really different from those of most people.

I also spoke with Sturgeon Bay Police Clerk Jenniece Hoiska about a phone call she received at work within days of the 9-11-2001 World Trade Center bombings in New York City. Hoiska stated she received a call from Steve Owens in which he was extremely upset and stated "nobody goes and kills Americans and gets away with it." Owens asked if Sturgeon Bay Police Department needed any help, stating "I should go get him myself," apparently referring to Osama bin Laden.

On 12-27-01 it was learned that a blood draw taken from [Tom Azinger] upon his arrival at the hospital after the stabbing revealed a blood alcohol concentration of 0.13%.

Source Document 3
Statements to Police by Steven Owens
December 25 & 26, 2001

A. First statement, dated 12-25-2001, 1:12 a.m. Three handwritten pages, transcribed (printed) by Sgt. Terry Vogel.

On today's date I woke up sometime before noon. I drank some water and coffee like I usually do. My roommate [Greg Hoefman] was already up. I huddled with Greg until approx. 4:00 p.m. when he left to go to his mother's house.

Approx. 15-20 minutes later [Tom Azinger] showed up at my house. He had with him a guitar and a backpack. Inside the backpack was a half-full bottle of Aristocrat Brandy. [Tom] said he wanted to sit and play the guitar and jam awhile. While he was there I changed all the strings on his guitar and tried to fix his bridge. While doing this we both consumed almost all of the brandy. I would consider myself very drunk by this time.

We started arguing about politics. I think they are all a bunch of fucking liars. We argued verbally for about 10 minutes. [Tom] told me I got it made because the government gives me $6,000 per year [SSDI payments].

At this point I told [Tom] to get the hell out of my house. I turned my back on him and I got struck over the head by an unknown object. I turned around and we began wrestling for a while. [Tom] got me in a headlock at one point. I began to get out of it and I got some distance from him. I saw him reach down for something but I'm not sure what it was. At this point I went into my bedroom and got my sword. I again hollered to him, "[Tom], get the fuck out of here." At least 3 times before I got back to him I hollered for him to get out of my house. I approached him within 4 feet and again told him to get out or I was going to stick you. He laughed at me and made an offensive move toward me. I then stuck him, but I

162

Document 3

didn't use a lot of pressure. As I stuck at him he grabbed my sword with his hand. I pulled the sword back and he began yelling at me as he backed away. It looked like he was going to get his guitar and leave. I threw the sword behind me and I left. I walked down the hill toward the highway. I think I was gone for about 1/2 hour. I came back home and was going to go to bed. At this point I was confronted by the police.

I have know [Tom Azinger] for about 15 years. We have gotten into 3 other physical fights. The last fight was about 2 or 3 years ago.

This statement was given by my own free will. I was read the Miranda rights by Sgt. Terry Vogel, which I understood and agreed to waive. This is a true and accurate statement to the best of my knowledge and was written by Sgt. Terry Vogel with my permission

[statement signed by Vogel and Owens]

B. Second statement, dated 12-26-2001, 10:14 a.m. Five hand-written pages, transcribed (printed) by Sgt. Terry Vogel.

I am writing this statement of my own free will and have been advised of my rights by Sgt. Terry Vogel, which I willingly waived.

This statement is a second voluntary statement I am giving and is written to help explain what occurred the evening of Dec. 24th.

Prior to the actual physical fight, I was sitting on the brown chair just finishing putting the strings on his guitar. [Tom] was sitting on the couch in my living room. We verbally argued for 10–15 minutes. We were arguing about terrorists. I was very drunk at this time, probably drunker than I have been in years and don't remember the exact details. I was getting a headache from his constant yelling and was getting very angered at him. I don't remember what he was saying but I got out of my chair past [Tom] and opened the [front] door. I walked back toward my chair past [Tom] and again told him to leave. My exact words were, "[Tom], get the fuck out of here."

Things then got physical and he attacked me. Everything got trashed during this fight and we both ended up on the carpet. He tried to get me in a chokehold and I knocked his arms away. He then got me in a headlock. I don't know how but I got out of the headlock. I started running away and did [sic] until I got hit on my neck or shoulder by an unknown object. It knocked me down. I then saw him reach for something so I ran to my room to get my sword. My sword was in a sheath next to my window. I took it out of the sheath and came back toward him, telling him to get out.

At this point I'm not mad, I'm more scared. I now confront him with the sword. I don't exactly remember because I was drunk but I held the sword with my right hand, putting the blade on my left forearm pointed toward him. He laughed at me and tried to lunge at me. [Tom] grabbed the sword with both hands approximately 6 in. from the tip and tried to get it away from me by pulling it toward him. I poked at him only once and I am sure the autopsy will show that. I pushed the sword at him like you would push a stick at someone to get him away from you. As soon a I felt some resistance, I backed off and pulled the sword back. As I pulled it back, he then let go of the sword. He said to me, "You fucker." He then turned around and walked out. He had his back to me and started walking away, holding his hand. I assumed he had cut his hands. I did not think the sword entered his body but thought it may have cut his shirt or coat. I watched him walk across the lawn, staggering. I yelled to him something like, "The door is open if you want to grab your shit."

After he left the house, I dropped the sword. I decided to leave to go for a walk. Before I left I put on my snowmobile suit, because I was thinking of walking to my mother's house. I also put my coat on over my snowmobile suit. My hat was in my jacket. I left my house within 15-20 seconds after [Tom] left. I walked behind my apartment to the business highway. From there I walked the business highway to Neenah St. toward the highway. I then crossed the highway. I got to the other side and decided it wasn't a good idea to go to my mother's house because I was drunk, so I decided to return.

On the way back I went past the fire station and behind Bayview Terrace [apartments]. I eventually came out by Neenah St. and Spruce Ct. I took kind of a haphazard route just kind of wandering around. I think it was behind the Bayview Terrace that I wrote in the snow with my finger the words ""U DIE! I'M AREADY [sic] DEAD. ThAX X!" I believe at that time I was thinking about nuclear war and asteroid impact (world destruction).

On the way back to my apartment, I waved at [Greg Hoefman] at the corner of Neenah and Spruce Ct. I then walked up toward the apartment. As soon as I saw the police, I stopped when they told me to freeze and get down [on the ground]. I told the police to shoot me because [Tom] was going to press charges and I was going to jail. I cooperated with the police.

I would also like to add that approximately 5 minutes after leaving my apartment, I threw up. This was caused by my drinking and the fact that I had gotten into a fight.

I give the officers permission to enter my apartment to search it.

The shotgun shell found in my pocket is a 20-gauge shell I made up myself 2–3 years ago. My intention with the shell was self-defense.

Approximately 5 years ago I purchased a 22-calibre handgun from Bob Warner for 400 dollars. My intent with the gun was for target practice. I would go by Brett Clothier's farm to do my shooting. The last time I was out there was 2 or 3 months ago with Brett. We used his gun during this shooting. My gun got lost about one year ago while I was in a swamp. At my residence I still have numerous bullets.

I have not taken any medications since September. I was off of it for approx. 7 years before that. Since off my medication I felt I have been tweaky. During 1995 or 1996, I was in flight school and did not take any medication at that time. I felt perfectly good during that time without medications because I was busy studying. The reason I stopped taking medications was because I didn't trust the doctors. The only doctor I trust is Dr. [name redacted here].

This is a true and accurate statement to the best of my knowledge and was written by Sgt. Terry Vogel of the Door Co. Sheriff's Dept. with my permission.

[statement signed by Vogel and Owens]

Source Document 4
First Drawing of Crime Scene
by Steven Owens

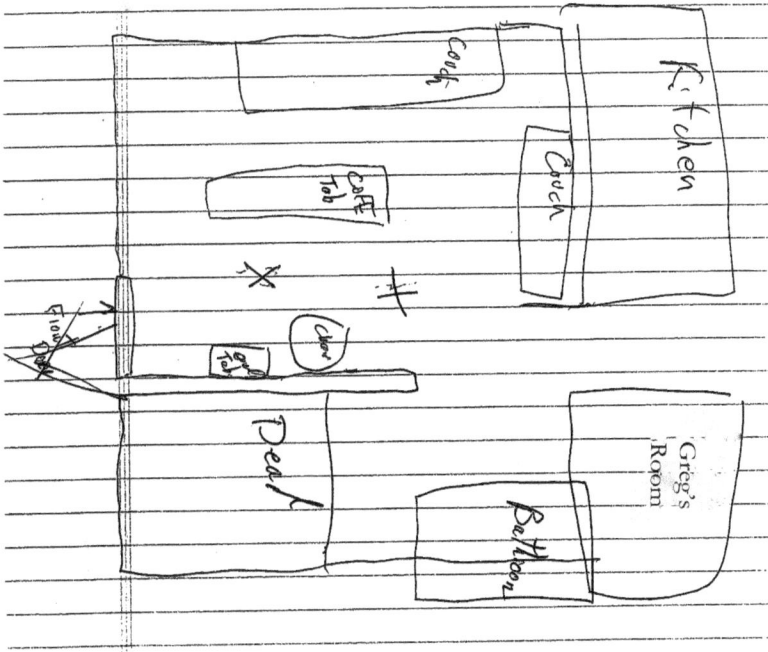

Drawing during first police interview (Dec. 25), about four hours after stabbing. The left "X" shows position of victim (near front door), the right "X" shows position of Owens. The two were standing between a coffee table and a chair and table. Much of the furniture was broken during a fight between the two men, briefly before the stabbing.

Source Document 5
Second Drawing of Crime Scene
by Steven Owens

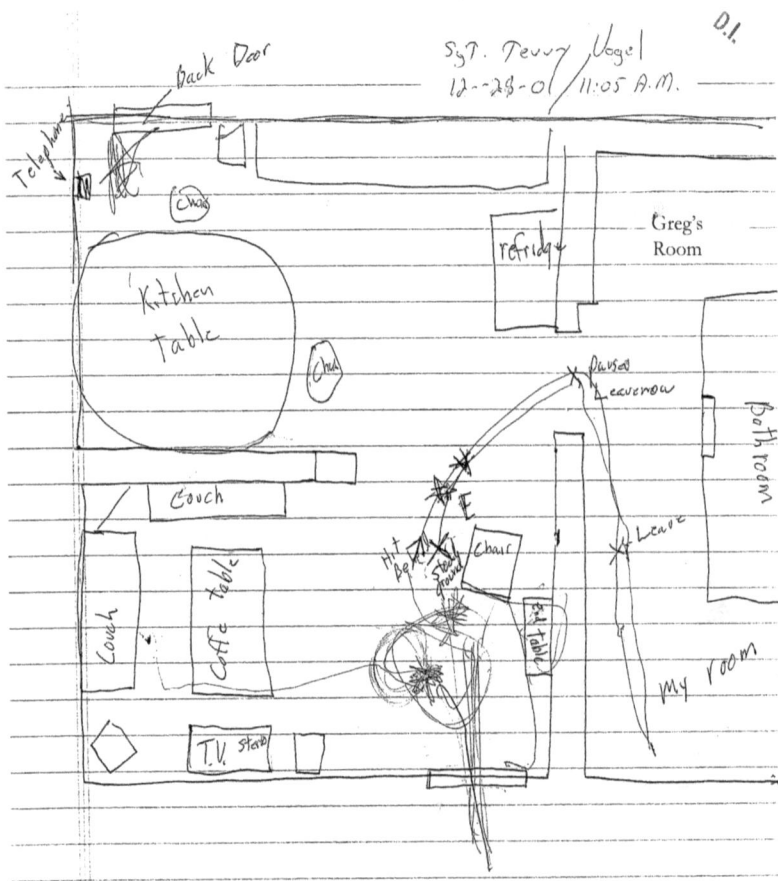

Drawing during second police interview (Dec. 26), about 18 hours after the first drawing. Note the richness of this drawing, compared to the first drawing. "Hit" indicates where Owens said he was hit on the back of the head, while trying to walk away from victim. See pathway from living room to Owens's bedroom down the hallway. At two points marked by "Xs," Owens says he shouted for victim to "Leave!" and "Leave now!" Between words "Hit" and "Chair" is "stood ground," indicating where Owens stood just prior to infliction of the sword wound.

Acknowledgments

I am making the unusual decision to start by acknowledging people who chose *not* to contribute to the writing of *Fatal Sword*. When I began my research for the book, I poured over public records, seeking as much information as was available. More importantly, I tried to locate people who personally knew Tom Azinger or Steve Owens at any point during their lives.

I had good luck identifying key people but terrible success connecting with them. Dozens of letters, phone calls, and electronic messages were unreturned. Sometimes I received brief replies, such as, "What is this about?" My honest answer typically resulted in little or no help. Violent crime and tragic death happen in all communities, but residents of small towns, like Sturgeon Bay, might me especially protective of their friends and even their community's reputation. An outsider comes with a slew of questions, and their guard goes up.

Here is an example of what I encountered. Chris* attended four years of high school with Tom Azinger, both graduating from Sevastopol High School in 1983. In a graduating class of only about sixty students, surely Chris and Tom had known each other, probably were in several classes together, or at least saw each other regularly in the school hallways. There is more. While Chris and Tom were still in grade school, Chris's aunt married Tom's brother, and years later they had a child. The aunt was close to Tom and was an official witness at his first marriage ceremony. Chris and Tom very likely attended the same family gatherings and celebrations.

I sent Chris a letter, introducing myself and describing my book project. With my poor track record I wasn't surprised to receive no response. Hesitantly I approached Chris at a place of employment. As quietly as I could, I introduced myself, mentioned the letter I sent, and asked for some insight into Tom—any help at all. Chris politely declined, responding, "I didn't really know him that well."

Most of all, I hoped to speak to family members themselves, those who knew Tom and Steve most intimately. I have the greatest respect, and sympathy, for the loved ones of Tom Azinger. Generally they continue to reside in Door County, where they surely face regular reminders of his violent death. I understand their probable angst over the writing of this book and their unwillingness to contribute. Still, I hope they choose to read *Fatal Sword* and realize it is, in part, a tribute to Tom.

~ ~

There were many people who gave freely of their time and expertise, and I gratefully acknowledge their assistance and encouragement.

Cindy and Deana Raynier offered fond memories of Steve Owens as a young adult. Their perspectives and insights were crucial to my understanding a side of Steve that few people knew. I wish I had met Bob Raynier, who died in 2004 from complications of syringomyelia.

Patrick Jeanquart provided many humorous and heart-warming stories of his friendship with Steve Owens. Anyone who remembers carefree days of adolescence with a best friend will surely appreciate Patrick's stories.

Carl Whitford openly shared insights into Steve Owens during Steve's difficult time after returning to Sturgeon Bay from the air force. Carl also offered firsthand information about important events in the case of David Dellis.

Dean Cuyler generously shared the good times he experienced with Tom Azinger and Steve Owens.

Former students and staff at Sevastopol and Sturgeon Bay schools provided valuable insights into student life in the 1970s and 1980s.

Acknowledgments

John Behringer was a classmate and science lab partner of Steve Owens's during high school, and the two kept in touch for a few years after graduation. John's input into Steve's character and experiences was especially valuable.

Mike Hoeft, a long-time news reporter, covered dozens of Door County criminal trials, including the trial of Steve Owens. His memories of the courtroom events and his insights into small-town justice were quite helpful.

James Downey, who has practiced law in Door County for many years, provided helpful information about policing and judicial processes in criminal cases. Matthew Van Grinsven, a current law student, attended the Owens trial and offered valuable observations of the courtroom events, as well as views on criminal prosecution.

Officers and personnel of the Sturgeon Bay Police Department and Door County Sheriff's Office were extremely pleasant and helpful. I appreciate their adherence to the letter and spirit of the Wisconsin Open Records Law.

Three law enforcement officers deserve special mention. Thomas J. Baudhuin and Terry J. Vogel did their best to answer all of my questions in an open and honest manner. Both are now retired, but it is obvious that their dedication to law enforcement continues. I asked Arleigh R. Porter to rack his memory for details of the Owens case, and he did his best. He also directed me to important documents available to the public.

Judge Peter C. Diltz, now retired, responded in length to my several detailed questions. His views about judicial processes in general and about challenges specific to the Owens case were interesting and invaluable. As he noted, "there is only one judicial perspective on a case." I am grateful he offered me a part of his.

Tim Funnell politely returned my phone call. When I told him about my project, I expected him to hang up on me but, to his credit, he listened. I asked pointed questions, and his answers were guarded, perhaps understandably so. To almost every query he enjoined me to *read the trial transcript!* I did, all 1913 pages, plus supplementary materials. Tim's was good advice, indeed.

Michael K., a recent resident of the apartment on E. Spruce Court, couldn't have been more helpful. I knocked on his front door, not knowing what or whom to expect. When I explained my project, he graciously invited me in. Did he know about the tragedy in his apartment years before? "I've heard some rumors," he admitted. Standing in the small living room where the battle on Christmas Eve took place, I began to tell the story. Then I asked to tour the apartment. It was an interesting experience for both of us. Though I had previously seen diagrams of the apartment, it was *much* smaller than I had imagined.

A friend of Lorine Azinger's discreetly described Lorine's personal qualities and experiences, including the excruciating days immediately following the death of her son Tom.

Ricky Hoefman and Becki Hoefman agreeably described their perspectives and longtime memories of Tom and Steve. I am greatly appreciative, especially since our discussions probably were emotionally difficult for them.

I was able to speak to Greg Hoefman only once, but his insights about Tom and Steve were heartfelt and meaningful. Neither of them could have asked for a better friend.

Julie Kudick and John Borrowman III, authors themselves, were invaluable as manuscript readers. Each provided unique insights and recommendations, and I'm grateful for their continuing support.

My constant companion supplied not only her usual, steadfast encouragement but also valuable guidance on all parts of the project. She read every version of the manuscript, always offering the "reader's perspective." Sometimes I didn't like her advice but I always trusted her judgment. She was with me from the first word of the first draft to the final punctuation mark of the book, so she deserves its last two words: Peggy Dodd.

About the Author

David K. Dodd, a former psychologist, now writes books of true crime. Previously he wrote *Furnace Murder,* coauthored with Harvey W. Rowe. It tells the true story of a horrific murder that occurred in 1948 in Sturgeon Bay, Wisconsin. He has also written three novels: *Star Shooting, Star Dawning,* and *NOY World.* Prior to his recent move to St. Louis, Missouri, Dodd lived in the small town of Fish Creek, Wisconsin, in the heart of northern Door County.

His author website is: www.DavidKDodd.com.

www.ingramcontent.com/pod-product-compliance
Lightning Source LLC
Chambersburg PA
CBHW052042090426
42739CB00010B/2010